THE HAPPY
HOME BAKER
Cookbook

Elegant and
Fun Sweets
Made Simple

RIE
@happyhomebaker

Marshall Cavendish
Cuisine

Editor: Lo Yi Min
Designer: Bernard Go Kwang Meng
Photographer: Rie

© 2019 Marshall Cavendish International (Asia) Private Limited

Published by Marshall Cavendish Cuisine
An imprint of Marshall Cavendish International

A member of the
Times Publishing Group

Other Marshall Cavendish Offices:
Marshall Cavendish Corporation, 99 White Plains Road, Tarrytown NY 10591-9001,
USA • Marshall Cavendish International (Thailand) Co Ltd, 253 Asoke, 12th Floor,
Sukhumvit 21 Road, Klongtoey Nua, Wattana, Bangkok 10110, Thailand •
Marshall Cavendish (Malaysia) Sdn Bhd, Times Subang, Lot 46, Subang Hi-Tech
Industrial Park, Batu Tiga, 40000 Shah Alam, Selangor Darul Ehsan, Malaysia

Marshall Cavendish is a registered trademark of Times Publishing Limited

National Library Board, Singapore Cataloguing-in-Publication Data

Name(s): Yasaki, Rie.
Title: The happy home baker cookbook : elegant and fun sweets made simple / Rie.
Description: Singapore : Marshall Cavendish Cuisine, 2019.
Identifier(s): OCN 1107057168 | ISBN 978-981-48-4156-6 (paperback)
Subject(s): LCSH: Cake. | Cookies. | Baking. | LCGFT: Cookbooks.
Classification: DDC 641.8653--dc23

Printed in Singapore

To Mum, who helped me discover
the joys of baking from a young age.

CONTENTS

INTRODUCTION

I became fascinated with baking at a young age, even though it was not something that came naturally to me. Once, I tried to bake a birthday cake for myself using a recipe from a baking book given to me by my mother. I enjoyed the whole process thoroughly, but the cake was a miserable failure! Instead of being disheartened, I was interested in understanding the science behind each recipe and determined to produce successful bakes. Slowly but surely, I learnt how to bake through trial and error. In fact, while I was still in school, I even took on part-time jobs related to baking, working at a bread shop as well as a cake cafe. I was delighted whenever I was asked to assist in the kitchen — I would do my best to observe and apply what I had learnt when I got home.

Over time, I have found that sweets with simple recipes are more likely to be made often because of how easy it is to prepare them. When I moved to Singapore, the ingredients and equipment I was used to baking with in Japan were less readily available. So I embraced the challenge of baking with what I had and have since developed new techniques to simplify recipes. I've included many of these recipes in this book. Whether you are an experienced home baker wanting to whip up something quickly, or someone new to baking looking to build confidence, there will be something to suit your tastes. There are also recipes that take a little more time, especially those that are creative takes on classic cakes and flavours, but they are well worth the effort. As all the recipes come with step-by-step photographs for clarity, you will find that they are easy to follow. When baking is uncomplicated, you are able to appreciate the process of baking more.

Apart from enjoying delicious aromas wafting from the oven, I like sharing what I bake with my family and friends. To me, a home-baked good is a special treat because someone went the extra mile to prepare it from scratch. It could be meant as a gift on a special day, dessert at a dinner party, or simply an afternoon treat with coffee or tea — this collection has something perfect for every occasion. I hope that baking these treats will make you happy and also brighten someone else's day.

ACKNOWLEDGEMENTS

Even as I type these words of thanks, I can't quite believe that I have written a cookbook. I never imagined that I would become a cookbook author, so I'm still pinching myself occasionally to make sure that this is not a dream.

Writing this cookbook was a gratifying experience. Doing research and organising information clearly in every recipe have made me a better baker and writer. From the bottom of my heart, I would like to thank the people who have played a role in making this book a reality.

Mum, thank you for showing me the pleasures of baking when I was a child. I did not think then that it would become one of my favourite things in life. I still love the simple cookies, puddings and Japanese sweets you've taught me to make.

My grandfather, thank you for sharing your cooking skills and creating fun experiences in the kitchen with me. If I did not have all those lovely moments with you, I wouldn't enjoy baking as much as I do now.

My husband, for being the most patient and unflappable person in the world. Thank you for encouraging me to get my ideas down on paper and helping to check the accuracy of my writing. Writing this book has been a challenge, and you were always happy to lend a listening ear or give advice whenever I needed it, no matter how busy you were. My book would be empty without your continuous encouragement. I hope you look back on this challenge as one that created many good memories.

My wonderful friend Bu, thank you for sharing your ideas and tasting my new sweets. Your favourable comments always make me smile.

Special thanks to the team that helped to put this together and provided me with this opportunity to share some of what I love with others; in so doing, you've allowed me to develop and grow.

EQUIPMENT

Thermometer To execute these recipes with precision, you will need to take temperatures, and a digital probe thermometer will give you the best results.

The temperature at the centre of an oven might not match the temperature on the dial simply because the probe in the oven is not in the centre! An oven thermometer is an inexpensive tool that can save you future headaches. Once you take the temperature of the centre of your oven, you will know if the dial is inaccurate and, if so, how to adjust your baking temperatures accordingly.

Digital Scale This might be the most important equipment in making sweets and baking, as measuring the ingredients inaccurately is one of the biggest mistakes. Get a digital scale that can be set to grams and has a tare function to deduct the

weight of the bowl or plate. You can also use it to measure liquids like water, milk and juice, when 1 gram = 1 millilitre.

Mixing Bowls Rather than buying a set of mixing bowls of various sizes, get a few 0.7-litre to 3.5-litre stainless steel bowls, and at least one medium glass bowl. Stay away from aluminium, however, because acidic ingredients will react with the metal and change the flavour of your food.

Whisk Sure, you can use a wire whisk to beat a few eggs, but it's handy for other things too. In particular, it's one of the best tools for mixing dry ingredients together thoroughly and it's also great for stirring together a home-made custard.

Stand Mixer The ultimate mixer for anyone who bakes is, of course, a stand mixer. For the last decade, I have used a well-worn but much-loved stand mixer because it has 10 speeds that make mixing, kneading and whipping a breeze. While you can use a hand mixer, this ensures a smooth mix with the push of a button.

Hand Mixer A stand mixer may not be for everyone, and in that case, a hand mixer will do the job just as well, with only a little bit of effort needed when it comes to holding the mixer. There are plenty of great hand mixers out there.

Immersion Blender This is a type of blender that's easy to use and clean. Immersion blenders are great for making ganache or pastry cream, or for incorporating ingredients, hot or cold, without having to transfer them to another vessel. Just immerse it in the liquid and let it work.

Food Processor Having a food processor is going to make chopping large quantities of nuts or chocolate a breeze. Pastry dough will come together in a snap; my favourite recipe for Danish pastry calls for cutting the butter into the dough with a food processor, and it always turns out amazing. Some shortcuts are meant to be taken!

Cake Tins/Silicone Moulds/Metal Cake Rings/Tart Tins and Rings There are tins of all shapes, sizes and materials on the market these days. My recipes show my personal favourites, but you will surely enjoy finding what works best for you.

Silicone Baking Mats These can be used in the oven or freezer. They provide a great non-stick surface that won't flap about in the oven the way parchment paper will. Plus, they are reusable. These mats come in a variety of sizes to fit both American and European baking trays, so be sure to get the size that matches your tray. There are also silicone baking mats printed with measures that you can use as a non-stick surface for rolling out your dough to the right size.

Baking Paper For saving costs and being environmentally friendly, I prefer to use reusable silicone baking mats. However, if you do not have silicone baking mats, these are widely available in supermarkets and baking supply shops.

Piping Bags and Tips Have small and medium piping bags on hand. Avoid canvas bags because fatty product such as buttercream may leak through the sides. When buying piping tips, it is better to buy a collection containing various sizes of one type rather than a single tip of each type. A collection of round tips and open star (where the prongs are straight and not curved toward the centre) tips will have you covered.

Flat Wire Rack This is indispensable as baked treats have to be cooled properly by letting air circulate around them. Wire racks are also useful when glazing cakes and cookies. Set the glazed items on a wire rack and let the excess glaze drip off.

Pots and Pans It is practical to have a wide variety of sizes, from a very small saucepan for cooking sugar to use in an Italian meringue, to a deep pot you can make caramel in without it foaming up and bubbling over the sides.

Other Small Utensils

Strainer/Sifter A mesh strainer with a handle can be used twofold — to strain and to sift. You can also use it to help in rubbing the skins off of toasted nuts. Look for two types of strainers: one with a fine mesh so that small particles like citrus zest can't pass through it, and one with a slightly wider mesh to sift almond powder.

Rubber Spatula Scrape bowls cleanly with a rubber spatula so as not to waste any bit of batter or ingredient. A heat-safe rubber spatula is ideal for making crème anglaise because you can scrape the bottom and corners of the pan while stirring.

Plastic Bowl Scraper While this is also good for scraping bowls clean, it is great tool for folding ingredients into a batter. Because there is no handle, you get a better feel for the batter's consistency and know when to stop folding.

Rolling Pin A rolling pin helps flatten out and shape everything from pie and pastry crust to cookie dough. For a beginner, the roller type (with handles on the side) is easier to use and requires less pressure than the rod type. Get a good-quality wooden rolling pin and it'll be the only one you ever need to buy.

Pastry Brush This is used for glazing your pastry with egg wash or milk, or for brushing pie pastry with melted butter. It's also good for brushing off excess icing sugar when decorating cakes. A brush with natural boar bristles is recommended.

Palette Knife/Offset Palette Knife These are used for spreading batters, and lifting and moving desserts and their components.

Serrated Kitchen Knife Use this for slicing through a cake horizontally, cutting off excess dough or trimming the edges of cream cakes. When you cut chilled cakes, warm the knife with hot water and clean the blade after each cut to get nice cross sections.

INGREDIENTS

Flour The interior structure of baked goods is provided by flour. For this reason, controlling the amount of protein (gluten) in your flour is extremely important. If you think about it in terms of architecture, you can see why we would want a sturdier structure for breads (more protein) and a softer or shorter structure for cakes and cookies (less protein). All-purpose flour is totally acceptable for your average baked good, but if you're baking bread, buy bread flour; if you're baking a special cake, buy cake flour. It makes all the difference. Store flour in airtight, moisture-proof containers on a cool, dark shelf or in the refrigerator.

Rice Flour *Komeko*, also known as rice powder, is a flour made of finely milled rice. Rice flour is a particularly good substitute for wheat flour. *Shiratamako* is a type of glutinous rice flour that has been further refined. *Joushinko* is a fine, non-glutinous rice flour that has been milled after being polished.

Almond Powder Although it is sometimes called almond flour, this isn't a type of milled flour. It is simply finely ground blanched almonds, which can also be made easily at home. Almond powder is the main ingredient in French macarons and it is commonly used for airy cakes as well as cookies. I normally use extra fine almond powder as it's easily sifted and mixed with other flours.

Caster Sugar Made from the juice of sugar cane or beets, this kind of sugar is finely granulated. It has been stripped of its natural molasses and can be further refined to look white. For baking, I prefer to use extra fine caster sugar.

Icing (Confectioners') Sugar This is sugar that has been ground into ultra-fine particles and combined with starch so that it doesn't cake in its packaging. Bakers use this in frosting and icing. A quick dusting of icing sugar always makes everything a little prettier too.

Baking Powder Made from cream of tartar, baking soda and starch, baking powder is a leavening agent, which causes the batter to rise. As it has a built-in acidic component (the cream of tartar), there is no need to add an acidic ingredient to the batter. Too much baking powder leaves a bitter taste, while too little results in a tough baked good with little volume.

Baking Soda Otherwise known as sodium bicarbonate, baking soda is used as a leavening agent in baking. As it is alkaline, adding too much of baking soda to a batter will result in a soapy-tasting and coarse product.

Salt It might seem out of place in recipes for sweet treats, but salt enhances sweetness. Adding salt also helps preserve the colour and flavour of flour. In bread, it controls the fermentation rate of yeast and strengthens the gluten in the dough.

Oil For baking, I recommend using a light-coloured and flavourless oil so that it does not impart additional flavour to the baked goods. I use *taihaku* (太白/white) sesame oil, which is colourless and mild in flavour. You can get it in Japanese grocery stores or supermarkets. Grape seed oil, which may be easier to find, is a fantastic substitute.

Unsalted Butter Use unsalted butter in baking unless your recipe specifies salted butter. If you're not going to use it all the time, you can easily freeze butter until you need it. While butter is used often in batters and dough, it is also added to frostings for a rich texture.

Whipping Cream This contains 33 to 36 per cent milk fat and is used for making whipped cream. It can also be used in recipes that call for heavy cream.

Milk Adding milk is one way to add moisture to a batter. Whole milk gives a richer flavour, but you can make a one-to-one substitution with low-fat milk to suit your preference.

Eggs Another all-round useful ingredient, eggs are used in cake batters to trap air as well as bind the ingredients together. I usually use large eggs (with the egg yolk weighing about 20 g and egg white about 40 g).

Amazake Made from fermented rice, this traditional Japanese drink is sweet and can be low in alcohol or alcohol-free. It can be used in desserts, salad dressings or smoothies as a natural sweetening agent.

Fruit Purée These are often sold sweetened and frozen, and will need to be thawed before using.

Sweetened Red Bean Paste There are two types of red bean paste: smooth and coarse. Either type is fine for the recipes in this book.

Baking Chocolate/Cocoa Powder I use Callebaut and Cacao Barry, but there are many brands of chocolate for baking. For cocoa powder, I like Valrhona's.

Vanilla Beans Vanilla is an aromatic flavouring made from the beans of the vanilla orchid. It enhances other flavours and adds sweetness. To obtain the seeds, slice open a vanilla bean pod lengthwise and scrape down each half. A good vanilla bean should be flexible and slightly moist.

Pure Vanilla Extract This is a pantry essential, made by adding macerated vanilla beans to an alcohol-water mixture. It is an easy way to add vanilla flavour to baked goods as it is easily incorporated into batters.

Gelatine/Agar Gelatine is available in a powdered or leaf (sheet) form. The recipes in this book call for gelatine leaf as I like the texture and it's more manageable. If you prefer, you may substitute it with gelatine powder of the same weight. Add gelatine powder into cold or room temperature water that is 4–5 times the amount of powder and leave it for 10 minutes before using. Agar has similar gelling properties as gelatine, but it is made from algae. Jelly made with agar has a firmer texture compared to jelly made with gelatine. Agar jelly can also set at room temperature.

BASIC RECIPES

Genoise Sponge

Makes a 15-cm round cake

15 g unsalted butter

1¹/₂ Tbsp milk

2 eggs (140 g)

1 egg yolk (15 g)

75 g caster sugar
  (extra fine)

20 g glucose

75 g cake flour, sifted

1   Preheat oven to 170°C. Line a 15-cm round cake tin.

2   Melt butter and milk in a heatproof bowl set over a pot of simmering water. Set aside in a pan filled with warm water to keep mixture warm.

3   In another clean heatproof bowl, combine eggs, egg yolk, sugar and glucose. Place over a pot of simmering water and whisk continuously until mixture reaches 40°C.

4   Remove from heat. Using an electric mixer with a whisk attachment, whisk on high speed until batter reaches the ribbon stage. When you lift the whisk, the batter should fall slowly and form ribbons that hold their shape.

5   Adjust speed to low and beat for 2 minutes until batter is smooth and thick. When a skewer is inserted into the centre of the bowl, it should stand on its own.

6   Using a spatula, fold flour into batter. Mix a small amount of batter into the melted butter mixture. Add this mixture to the remaining batter and fold in gently until combined and glossy.

7   Pour batter into prepared cake tin. Tap cake tin a few times against a hard surface to remove any bubbles.

8   Adjust oven to 165°C. Bake for 35 minutes.

9   Invert onto a wire rack and leave to cool in cake tin for a few minutes. Unmould, flip cake over and cover with a damp tea towel. Leave for a few hours to cool completely before slicing to use.

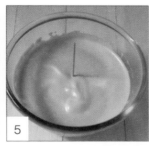

Basic Tart Shell

Makes an 18-cm tart shell

60 g unsalted butter, cut
  into cubes and chilled

37 g icing sugar

15 g almond powder
  (extra fine)

⅓ egg (20 g)

110 g cake flour

1 Place butter in the freezer while preparing the remaining ingredients.

2 Place icing sugar and almond powder in a food processor and pulse a few times to mix. Add butter cubes and pulse until mixture looks sandy.

3 Add egg and flour, then pulse until dough resembles clumpy breadcrumbs.

4 Transfer dough to a work surface covered with cling film and gently knead once or twice. Shape into a block about 2-cm thick. Wrap in cling film and refrigerate for 1−2 hours.

5 Place chilled dough between 2 large sheets of cling film. Gently tap dough 6 to 8 times with a rolling pin to flatten. Roll into a disc about 3- to 4-mm thick. Refrigerate for 10−15 minutes.

6 Drape dough over an 18-cm tart tin and gently press it in. Trim the edges, then poke holes in tart shell using a fork. Pipe or pour desired filling into tart, then refrigerate it while preheating oven.

7 Preheat oven to 170°C.

8 Bake for 30 minutes. Unmould and leave to cool on a wire rack.

Almond Cream

Makes about 180 g

45 g unsalted butter, at room temperature

45 g caster sugar (extra fine)

³/₄ egg (45 g)

45 g almond powder (extra fine)

8 g cornstarch

7 g custard powder

1 Using a spatula, beat butter and sugar together to form a paste.

2 Add egg and fold in gently. Add almond powder, followed by cornstarch and custard powder, mixing well after each addition.

3 Transfer to a piping bag and refrigerate until needed.

Italian Meringue

Makes about 145 g

100 g caster sugar (extra fine)

5¹/₂ tsp water

1 egg white (40 g)

1 In a small saucepan, combine sugar and water. Cook on medium-high heat until 117°C. Use a damp pastry brush to dissolve any sugar crystals on the sides of the pot.

2 While syrup cooks, place egg white in a clean mixing bowl and prepare an electric mixer with a whisk attachment. When syrup reaches 105°C, whisk egg white on high speed for 5–8 minutes until soft peaks form.

3 When syrup reaches 117°C, remove from heat and add gradually to egg white, keeping the electric mixer on high speed. The temperature of the mixture at this point should be 60°C.

4 Adjust speed to low and keep whisking until meringue reaches the desired consistency. Soft peaks are used for mousses and stiff peaks are best for buttercream and macarons.

KEEPING IT SIMPLE

Citron

Lemon Pound Cake

The zesty and bold flavours of this cake make it perfect for having with afternoon tea.

100 g cake flour

3 g baking powder

100 g unsalted butter,
  at room temperature

75 g caster sugar
  (extra fine)

2 eggs (100 g), at
  room temperature,
  lightly beaten

Zest of ½ lemon

A few drops of vanilla
  extract

Crushed pistachios
  and lemon zest for
  garnishing, as desired

Lemon syrup

4 tsp lemon juice,
  strained

4 tsp water

15 g caster sugar
  (extra fine)

Lemon glaze

100 g icing sugar

3—4 tsp lemon juice,
  strained

1   Prepare lemon syrup. Place all ingredients for lemon syrup
    in a microwave-safe bowl. Cover with cling film loosely and
    microwave at 500W for 1 minute until a syrup forms and boils.
    Set aside.

2   Preheat oven to 170°C. Line a 16-cm loaf tin.

3   Sift flour and baking powder together. Set aside.

4   Using an electric mixer with a whisk attachment, whisk butter
    and sugar on high speed until light and fluffy.

5   Add ¼ of eggs and stir to combine. Repeat with another ¼ of
    eggs. Add ⅓ of flour mixture and mix lightly. Add the remaining
    eggs in 2 equal portions, mixing well after each addition.

6   Add lemon zest and vanilla extract, then mix lightly to combine.

7   Using a spatula, fold in the remaining flour mixture. Add 15 g
    lemon syrup and fold in until batter looks glossy.

8   Pour batter into prepared loaf tin and smooth over the surface.
    Adjust oven to 160°C and bake for 35—40 minutes. After
    15 minutes, remove from oven and use a knife to slit the top of
    the loaf. Return to oven to continue baking.

9   Unmould cake onto a wire rack. Brush with the remaining lemon
    syrup and leave to cool.

10 Prepare lemon glaze. Place icing sugar in a bowl. Gradually add
    lemon juice and mix to form a pourable glaze. Spoon or pour
    glaze slowly over cake, letting glaze drip down the sides a little.
    Sprinkle with pistachios and lemon zest.

TIP
I highly recommend that you use organic lemons for this recipe.
If using regular lemons, wash them carefully to remove
any dirt and pesticides, as well as the waxy coating.

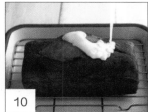

Custard Pudding

This is inspired by one of my
mother's favourite recipes,
tweaked for the adult palate.

5-cm length vanilla bean

400 ml milk

75 g caster sugar
(extra fine)

2 eggs (120 g)

1 egg yolk (20 g)

Caramel sauce

1 Tbsp water +
water for boiling

60 g caster sugar
(extra fine)

1 Prepare caramel sauce. In a saucepan, combine 1 Tbsp water and sugar over medium heat, stirring until sugar melts.

2 Adjust heat to high and cook without stirring until syrup turns a caramel colour. While syrup is heating, boil some water. When syrup is caramel in colour, remove from heat and add 5 tsp hot water. (Please be careful of steam rising from the saucepan.) Pour into a 650-ml oval pudding tin, tilting to spread caramel sauce evenly. Cover and refrigerate until needed.

3 Preheat oven to 150°C. Line a deep baking pan, which is large enough to hold the pudding tin, with a tea towel.

4 Split vanilla bean lengthwise. Using a paring knife, scrape vanilla seeds into a medium saucepan.

5 Add milk and sugar, then heat mixture over medium heat until 60°C. Meanwhile, place eggs and egg yolk in a large bowl and beat lightly.

6 When milk mixture is ready, add gradually to eggs and stir briskly to combine.

7 Strain pudding mixture twice and transfer to a bowl. Cover with a wet paper towel to remove any bubbles on the surface.

8 Slowly pour pudding mixture into pudding tin. Place pudding tin in prepared baking pan.

9 Pour hot water (about 65°C) into baking pan until it is halfway up the pudding tin's side. Cover baking pan with foil.

10 Bake for 60 minutes or until surface of pudding is set.

11 Remove from oven and leave to cool slightly. Refrigerate for 12 hours to chill completely.

TIP
To avoid getting a spongy texture and bland-tasting pudding, do not over heat the milk for the batter, as well as the water for the water bath.

Petits Gâteaux au Chocolat à L'orange

These mini cakes are an old favourite that has been perfectly portioned into individual servings. The key to this is mixing in the ingredients as lightly as you can.

28 g cake flour

18 g cocoa powder

25 g candied orange zest cut into 5-mm strips + more for decorating

30 g baking chocolate

23 g unsalted butter

18 g whipping cream + more for decorating

1½ egg yolk (30 g)

30 g caster sugar (extra fine)

Meringue

1½ egg whites (50 g)

30 g caster sugar (extra fine)

1 Preheat oven to 170°C. Line a baking tray and arrange six 7 x 4.5-cm oval mousse rings on top. Line the insides of each mousse ring. Fit a 12-mm round piping tip into a piping bag.

2 Sift flour and cocoa powder together twice. Add orange zest and mix to distribute zest evenly.

3 Melt chocolate, butter and whipping cream in a heatproof bowl set over a pot of simmering water. Set aside in a pan filled with warm water to keep chocolate mixture at 45°C.

4 Prepare meringue. Using an electric mixer with a whisk attachment, whisk egg white and caster sugar on high speed until soft peaks form. Refrigerate meringue until it is needed.

5 In another bowl, whisk egg yolk and sugar until pale. Add egg mixture to chocolate mixture and mix lightly using a spatula.

6 Add ⅓ of meringue to the batter and stir lightly to mix. Fold in flour mixture. Add the remaining meringue and fold it in, gently scraping the bottom of the bowl with the spatula as you go until the batter is a darker shade of brown.

7 Transfer batter to prepared piping bag and pipe equally into mousse rings. Fill each ring until ¾ full.

8 Bake for 18–20 minutes.

9 Remove from oven, then unmould and peel off baking paper immediately. Leave to cool on a wire rack.

10 Decorate with whipped cream and orange zest as desired.

TIP
Mixing the flour and orange zest together beforehand prevents the zest from sinking to the bottom while baking.

Le Canelés De Bordeaux

This rum-flavoured French pastry is simple yet sophisticated – a real crowd pleaser.

Makes 12 mini cakes

40 g unsalted butter

2 egg yolks (40 g)

2 eggs (120 g)

80 g cake flour

40 g cornstarch

150 g caster sugar
  (extra fine)

100 g light brown sugar

500 ml milk

1/2 vanilla bean

8 tsp rum

1   Make browned butter. Heat butter in a small saucepan over medium heat until it turns a light brown colour. Remove from heat, strain through a coffee filter or paper towel into a bowl and leave to cool. Portion out 25 g and set aside.

2   In a small bowl, beat egg yolks and eggs to combine. Set aside.

3   Sift cake flour, cornstarch and both sugars into a large bowl. Create a well in the centre of the mixture. Set aside.

4   Place milk in a saucepan. Split vanilla bean lengthwise. Using a paring knife, scrape vanilla seeds into saucepan. Add vanilla pod, then heat milk mixture until 60°C.

5   Remove from heat and strain milk slowly into flour mixture. Whisk until just incorporated. Be careful not to over-mix.

6   Whisk in egg mixture, followed by browned butter and rum. Mix until well combined.

7   Cover batter with cling film, ensuring that the cling film adheres to the surface of the batter. Refrigerate batter for 24–48 hours to let flavours and texture develop.

8   Preheat oven to 220°C. Line a baking tray. Brush 12 canelé moulds with butter.

9   Remove batter from the refrigerator. Whisk well before pouring into prepared moulds. Arrange filled moulds on baking tray.

10 Place tray on the upper rack and bake for 22 minutes. Transfer to the lower rack and bake at 180°C for 45 minutes.

11 Unmould and leave to cool on a wire rack.

Matcha Madeleines

This is my take on a classic French tea cake.

Makes 8 mini cakes

85 g unsalted butter

1½ eggs (77 g), at room temperature

67 g caster sugar (extra fine)

1 g salt

12 g honey

62 g cake flour

15 g almond powder (extra fine)

5 g matcha, sifted

3 g baking powder

1. Prepare 8 non-stick madeleine moulds. If using moulds that are not of the non-stick variety, brush them with butter, lightly dust with flour and tap out the excess. Refrigerate moulds until they are needed.

2. Melt butter in a heatproof bowl set over a pot of simmering water. Set aside in a pan filled with warm water to keep melted butter at 40°C.

3. In a medium bowl, beat eggs for 1 minute until frothy. Add sugar and salt, then beat for 1 minute. Add honey and mix until sugar is dissolved.

4. Sift flour, almond powder, matcha and baking powder into egg mixture and mix well.

5. Add melted butter to batter in portions, mixing well after each addition.

6. Cover batter with cling film, ensuring that the cling film adheres to the surface of the batter. Refrigerate batter for 1 hour.

7. Preheat oven to 230°C.

8. Using a spatula, stir batter to remove any bubbles, then transfer into a piping bag. Pipe batter equally into prepared moulds, filling each mould until $^4/_5$ full.

9. Bake at 230°C for 3 minutes. Adjust oven to 180°C and bake for another 3 minutes. Adjust oven to 160°C and bake for a further 3 minutes.

10. Unmould immediately and leave to cool on a wire rack.

TIP
Sifting the matcha once first prevents lumps in the batter.

Pandan Chiffon Cake

This fluffy and light cake is something I first tried after moving to Singapore. It is a rather popular cake in Southeast Asia.

40 g cake flour

30 g bread flour

3 g baking powder

3¹⁄₂ egg yolks (70 g)

35 g caster sugar
(extra fine)

30 g coconut oil, melted

1 Tbsp coconut milk

4 tsp pandan extract
(see below)

Whipped cream, as
desired

Gula melaka (palm sugar)
syrup, as desired

Pandan extract

80 g pandan leaves

200 ml water

Meringue

3¹⁄₂ egg whites
(140 g)

¹⁄₂ tsp lemon juice

35 g caster sugar
(extra fine)

1 Prepare pandan extract a day ahead. Wash pandan leaves carefully and trim off ends. Cut into 1-cm pieces.

2 Place 40 g pandan leaves and 100 ml water in a blender or food processor. Process for 10 seconds. Add the remaining pandan leaves and water, then process until a paste forms.

3 Transfer paste to a cheesecloth placed in a bowl. Gather the ends of the cloth and squeeze to extract the liquid. Alternatively, strain paste through a fine-mesh strainer. Pour pandan extract into a clean bottle and refrigerate overnight.

4 To use pandan extract, carefully drain away the liquid on top, taking only the thicker portion that settled at the bottom.

5 Preheat oven to 170°C. Prepare two 12-cm tube cake tins.

6 Sift both flours and baking powder together twice. Set aside.

7 In a medium bowl, beat egg yolks and sugar until pale. It should have the texture of mayonnaise.

8 Pour coconut oil gradually into egg yolk mixture, whisking continuously until emulsified. Add coconut milk and pandan extract and mix to combine. Add flour mixture and mix well. Set aside.

9 Prepare meringue. Using an electric mixer with a whisk attachment, whisk egg whites, lemon juice and ¹⁄₃ of sugar in a clean mixing bowl until foamy. Gradually add the remaining sugar, whisking continuously until firm peaks form. Switch to a hand whisk and whisk until meringue is smooth.

10 Add ¹⁄₃ of meringue to the batter and use a whisk to stir 20 times. Switch to a spatula and fold in the remaining meringue in 2 equal portions.

11 Pour equally into prepared cake tins. Dredge a wooden skewer through the batter to release any bubbles. Bake for 25 minutes.

12 Remove from oven and invert onto a wire rack. Leave to cool completely in cake tin.

13 Unmould to slice and serve with whipped cream and *gula melaka* syrup.

Soufflé Cheesecake

This cheesecake is so light and fluffy, it melts in your mouth.

15-cm round genoise sponge slice, 1.5-cm thick (see page 19)

150 g cream cheese

68 g mascarpone cheese

165 g plain unsweetened yoghurt

2 egg yolks (40 g)

25 g cornstarch

150 ml milk

2 egg whites (80 g)

100 g caster sugar (extra fine)

1 Preheat oven to 200°C. Grease a 15-cm cake tin. Line the base and sides of the cake tin, ensuring that the baking paper lining the sides of the tin has a height of 8 cm. Wrap the base of the cake tin with aluminium foil. Prepare a deep baking pan that is large enough to hold the cake tin.

2 Place round genoise sponge slice in prepared cake tin. Set aside.

3 Soften cream cheese by microwaving for 2 minutes at 200W. Add mascarpone cheese and mix well.

4 Add yoghurt a tablespoonful at a time and mix well before beating in egg yolks. Add cornstarch and mix to combine.

5 Gradually add milk, stirring constantly until batter is smooth. Strain batter and set aside.

6 Using an electric mixer with a whisk attachment, whisk egg whites until they start to foam. Gradually add sugar and whisk lightly to incorporate. The mixture should still be a little runny, so do not overbeat.

7 Using a spatula, fold $\frac{1}{3}$ of egg white mixture into batter. Add the remaining egg white mixture in 2 equal portions, mixing well after each addition.

8 Pour batter into prepared cake tin.

9 Place cake tin in prepared baking pan. Pour hot water (about 60°C) into baking pan until the water is halfway up the cake tin's side.

10 Adjust oven to 190°C and bake for 13 minutes. Adjust oven to 150°C, rotate cake tin 180° **and bake** for 30−35 minutes.

11 Leave cheesecake in the oven with the door slightly ajar for 30 minutes. Remove onto a wire rack and leave to cool completely in cake tin. Refrigerate to chill and unmould just before serving.

TIP

For a matcha flavoured version, use a matcha or cocoa sponge cake for the base. Substitute 25 g cornstarch with a mixture of 8 g matcha and 21 g cornstarch.

2

4a

4b

5a

5b

6a

6b

8

Rum Balls

These are so easy to make. I usually use leftover sponge cake, such as the excess from cutting out a round sponge slice. This way, I won't waste anything, and I get another treat!

20 g almond powder (extra fine)

40 g dark baking chocolate, roughly chopped

150 g sponge cake of your desired flavour

30 g rum-soaked raisins

1 Tbsp rum

Cocoa powder for dusting (optional)

Flaky salt for sprinkling (optional)

Coating

80 g dark baking chocolate

7 g coconut oil

1. Spread almond powder on a baking tray and roast at 120°C for 5 minutes. Melt chocolate in a heatproof bowl set over a pot of simmering water. Set aside almond powder and chocolate.

2. Place sponge cake in a food processor and pulse a few times.

3. Add almond powder and chocolate, then pulse to mix.

4. Add $1/2$ of rum raisins and $1/2$ of rum, and pulse to combine. Add the remaining rum raisins and rum, then pulse until mixture is crumbly.

5. Shape mixture into 10 similar-sized balls. Arrange on a baking tray, cover with cling film and refrigerate for at least 1 hour to firm up.

6. Prepare coating. Melt chocolate and oil in a heatproof bowl set over a pot of simmering water. Once melted and combined, remove mixture from heat and leave to cool until room temperature (25°C).

7. Line a baking tray with mini baking cups. Using a skewer or teaspoon, dip a rum ball into the coating. Place in a mini baking cup. Repeat to coat all balls.

8. If the remaining coating starts to set, place bowl over a pot of simmering water to warm up until coating is slightly runny again. Transfer to a small piping bag and pipe onto rum balls to decorate as desired.

9. Dust with cocoa powder or sprinkle with flaky salt if desired. Leave to set before serving.

TIP

If rum-soaked raisins are unavailable, make some with 50 g raisins and 80 ml rum. If raisins are coated in oil, scald them in hot water, then drain and pat dry thoroughly. Place raisins in a sterilised jar and add rum. Cover and leave to soak for more than 1 day before using.
For a slightly sweeter coating, use 40 g milk chocolate and 40 g dark chocolate instead.

MY COOKIE BOX

Piping Cookies

This is an extremely versatile cookie as it can be piped into various shapes. Exercise your creativity and make these any way you wish.

Plain dough

80 g unsalted butter,
  at room temperature

50 g icing sugar

A pinch of salt

$^1/_3$ egg (20 g), at room
temperature

125 g cake flour,
  sifted

Cocoa dough

90 g unsalted butter,
  at room temperature

40 g icing sugar

A pinch of salt

$^1/_3$ egg (20 g), at room
temperature

108 g cake flour,
  sifted

12 g cocoa powder,
  sifted

Coating

50 g milk chocolate

Freeze-dried
  raspberries, as
  desired

Chopped pistachios,
  as desired

1   Preheat oven to 170°C. Line a baking tray. Fit a star piping tip into a piping bag.

2   Prepare plain dough. Place butter, sugar and salt in a bowl and mix using a spatula.

3   Switch to an electric mixer with a whisk attachment and whisk for about 5 minutes until fluffy and pale.

4   Add $^1/_2$ of egg and whisk until incorporated. Add the remaining egg and whisk until stiff peaks form.

5   Using a spatula, fold in flour until incorporated and the dough no longer sticks to the spatula.

6   Transfer to prepared piping bag and pipe shapes onto baking tray.

7   Bake for 15 minutes. Leave to cool on a wire rack.

8   Follow steps 1–7 to prepare cocoa cookies. Fold cocoa powder and flour into batter.

9   Prepare coating. Melt chocolate in a heatproof bowl set over a pot of simmering water. Dip one end of each cookie into chocolate to coat, then place on a wire rack. Sprinkle with raspberries and pistachios before leaving to set. Repeat to coat cookies as desired.

Cheddar Cookies

This is a savoury cookie that is light and goes well with wine.

70 g cake flour

15 g bread flour

50 g unsalted butter, at room temperature

10 g caster sugar (extra fine)

A pinch of salt

14 g egg, combined with 8 g Greek yoghurt, at room temperature

43 g cheddar, freshly grated + more for topping

Pink peppercorns for topping, as desired

1   Combine both flours in a bowl and set aside.

2   In another bowl, beat butter lightly. Add sugar and salt, then mix well until incorporated.

3   Add egg mixture gradually, stirring constantly until ingredients are combined.

4   Add cheddar and flour mixture, then mix until mixture resembles clumpy breadcrumbs.

5   Lightly knead mixture by using a spatula or the heel of your palm to smear the dough against the bowl. Do this until a pliable dough forms.

6   On a lightly floured surface, roll dough into a 5-mm thick sheet. Wrap in cling film and refrigerate for 2 hours.

7   Preheat oven to 160°C. Line a baking tray.

8   Cut dough into triangles, each about 3 x 4.5-cm, and arrange on prepared baking tray. Top with cheddar and pink peppercorns.

9   Bake for 15—20 minutes until edges are slightly golden. Leave to cool on a wire rack.

> **TIP**
> Cake flour may be substituted with all-purpose flour. Chill the cut cookie dough in the refrigerator while waiting for the oven to preheat.

Damier Cookies
Checquerboard Cookies

This cookie has a beautiful, clean pattern, and the purple adds a whimsical touch.

Makes about 15 large cookies and 30 small cookies

75 g unsalted butter, at room temperature

60 g icing sugar, sifted

A pinch of salt

2¹/₂ tsp milk

Plain dough mix

64 g cake flour

14 g almond powder

Purple dough mix

55 g cake flour

11 g almond powder

13 g sweet potato powder

1　Prepare plain dough mix. Sift flour and almond powder together. Set aside.

2　Prepare purple dough mix. Sift flour, almond powder and sweet potato powder together. Set aside.

3　Place butter, sugar and salt in a bowl and mix using a spatula.

4　Gradually add milk to butter mixture while stirring continuously. Mix until incorporated, then divide batter equally into 2 bowls.

5　Add plain dough mix to the first bowl in 2 equal portions, mixing well after each addition.

6　Add purple dough mix to the other bowl in 2 equal portions, mixing well after each addition.

7　Cover dough with cling film and refrigerate for 1 hour.

8　Divide plain dough into 3 equal portions. On a surface covered with cling film, roll each portion into a 4-cm wide rectangular block of 1-cm thickness. Cut each block lengthwise into four small strips, each 1-cm wide. Repeat to roll out and cut purple dough.

9　Pair each strip of plain dough with a strip of purple dough, stacking one on top of the other. To make a small cookie log, gently press 2 stacks together, ensuring that dough colours are alternating. Repeat to make 2 small cookie logs. To make a large cookie log, gently press 4 stacks together and place on top of another 4 stacks, ensuring that dough colours are alternating. Refrigerate cookie logs for 2 hours.

10　Preheat oven to 160°C. Line a baking tray. Cut cookie logs into 0.7-mm thick slices and arrange on prepared baking tray.

11　Bake for 13 minutes. Leave in oven for 15 minutes before removing onto a wire rack to cool.

TIP
For clean edges, I use a pizza cutter and ruler to cut the dough.

8a

8b

9a

9b

10

Diamantes

We call these cookies 'diamantes' as their sugar coating resembles diamonds.

Fine grain caster sugar for coating

Water or egg white for brushing

Cocoa almond dough

45 g unsalted butter, cut into cubes and chilled

20 g icing sugar

12 g cocoa powder

48 g cake flour

15 g almond powder (extra fine)

20 g sliced almonds

1/2 egg yolk (10 g)

Earl Grey dough

45 g unsalted butter, cut into cubes and chilled

20 g icing sugar

60 g cake flour

15 g almond powder (extra fine)

2 g Earl Grey tea leaves, finely ground and sifted

1/2 egg yolk (10 g)

Matcha dough

45 g unsalted butter, cut into cubes and chilled

20 g icing sugar

3 g matcha

57 g cake flour

15 g almond powder (extra fine)

1/2 egg yolk (10 g)

1   Prepare cocoa almond dough. Place all ingredients except sliced almonds and egg yolk into a clean resealable plastic bag. Seal bag and shake vigorously to mix ingredients. Freeze for 1 hour.

2   Prepare a 15 x 30-cm sheet of baking paper.

3   Place chilled dough mixture into a food processor and pulse until clumpy. Transfer to a bowl, then add sliced almonds and mix gently using a spatula. Add egg and mix to form a pliable dough.

4   Transfer dough to a work surface covered with cling film. Working quickly, roll dough into a 30-cm log. Wrap with prepared baking paper and roll lightly to make log surface smooth. Freeze for 30 minutes.

5   Preheat oven to 170°C. Line a baking tray.

6   Place sugar for coating in a large tray. Unwrap chilled dough and brush lightly with water before rolling in tray to coat with sugar.

7   Cut into 1.5-cm thick slices and arrange on prepared baking sheet. Bake for 12−14 minutes.

8   Remove onto a wire rack and leave to cool.

9   Follow steps 1−8 to prepare Earl Grey and matcha flavours. For both flavours, place all ingredients except egg yolk into a clean resealable plastic bag.

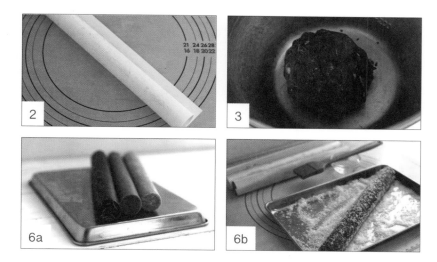

Florentines

Florentines are ubiquitous in Europe. These are made with a shortcrust base and candied toasted almonds

Makes 20–25 cookies

Cookie dough

105 g cake flour, sifted

30 g icing sugar

1 g baking powder

A small pinch of salt

55 g unsalted butter, cut into cubes and chilled

⅓ egg (20 g)

Nougat

80 g, sliced almonds, toasted until lightly browned

45 g unsalted butter

45 g whipping cream

65 g caster sugar

20 g glucose

20 g honey

1 Spread sliced almonds for nougat on a baking tray and toast at 170°C for 3–5 minutes until lightly browned. Set side to cool.

2 Prepare cookie dough. Line a 20-cm square baking tin.

3 Place flour, sugar, baking powder, salt and butter in a food processor bowl. Refrigerate for 15 minutes.

4 Pulse chilled ingredients a few times. Add egg and pulse to form a pliable dough.

5 Transfer dough to a work surface covered with cling film and roll into a 20-cm square. Place on prepared baking tray, cover with cling film and refrigerate for at least 3 hours, preferably overnight.

6 Preheat oven to 180°C. Use a fork to prick holes across the dough.

7 Bake for 10–15 minutes until lightly browned. Remove from oven and set aside in baking tray. Adjust oven to 170°C.

8 Prepare nougat. In a medium pot over medium heat, combine butter, whipping cream, sugar, glucose and honey until mixture reaches 115°C. Remove from heat and stir in sliced almonds.

9 Pour over cookie and spread almonds evenly.

10 Bake for 15–20 minutes until nougat is caramel in colour.

11 Leave to cool slightly before flipping florentine so that cookie layer is on top. Cut into 20–25 slices. Transfer to a wire rack to cool completely.

> **TIP**
> Be organised! Prepare the nougat while the cookie dough is in the oven; this saves time and helps with assembling the florentine more quickly. To cut florentine cleanly into smaller pieces, do so while it is still warm.

1

5a

5b

8

9

Herbes

Herb Cheese Cookies

These go well with hearty soups. Using fresh herbs instead of dried ones will give these cookies a brighter pop of colour.

Makes about 30 cookies

8 g egg, at room temperature

8 g plain unsweetened yoghurt

80 g unsalted butter, at room temperature

16 g caster sugar (extra fine)

65 g cake flour

15 g bread flour

8 g Parmigiano–Reggiano (or parmesan), grated

5 g herb of your choice (basil, rosemary, oregano), finely chopped

1 In a bowl, combine egg and yoghurt. Set aside.

2 In another bowl, beat butter lightly. Add sugar and mix well until incorporated.

3 Add egg mixture gradually, stirring constantly until ingredients are combined.

4 Add both flours, cheese and herb. Mix until mixture resembles clumpy breadcrumbs.

5 Lightly knead mixture by using a spatula or the heel of your palm to smear the dough against the bowl. Do this until a pliable dough forms.

6 Transfer dough to a work surface covered with cling film and roll into a 5-mm thick sheet. Wrap in cling film and refrigerate for 2 hours.

7 Preheat oven to 160°C. Line a baking tray.

8 Cut dough into rectangles, each about 1 x 7-cm, and arrange on prepared baking tray.

9 Bake for 18–19 minutes until golden brown. Leave to cool on a wire rack.

TIP
Cake flour may be substituted with all-purpose flour.
If Parmigiano-Reggiano is unavailable, use a non-Italian parmesan cheese or substitute with a hard, aged cheese that is good for grating.

Lemon and White Chocolate Shortbread

This shortbread is so light and crumbly, it practically melts in your mouth. Keep an eye on the cookies while they bake to make sure they don't brown too much.

Makes about 20 cookies

100 g unsalted butter, cut into cubes and chilled

150 g cake flour

100 g *komeko* (rice flour)

60 g icing sugar

A pinch of salt

Zest of 1 organic lemon

60 g white baking chocolate, finely chopped

2 Tbsp soy milk

1 Place all ingredients except chocolate and soy milk into a clean resealable plastic bag. Seal bag and shake vigorously to mix ingredients. Freeze for 1 hour.

2 Place chilled mixture and chocolate in a food processor and pulse until clumpy.

3 Transfer mixture to a bowl. Add soy milk in portions, working quickly with your hands to mix until each addition is incorporated and a dough forms. Wrap in cling film and refrigerate for 15 minutes.

4 Transfer dough to a work surface covered with cling film and roll into a 1.5-cm thick block. Wrap in cling film and freeze for 1 hour.

5 Preheat oven to 130°C. Line a baking tray.

6 Using a sharp knife, cut dough into 2 x 7-cm rectangles. Use a toothpick or skewer to prick holes down the length of each rectangle.

7 Arrange on prepared baking tray and bake for 45 minutes. Leave shortbread in oven for 15 minutes before removing to cool on a wire rack.

TIP
The soy milk should be added gradually because how much you need to hydrate the rice flour depends on the brand that you use.

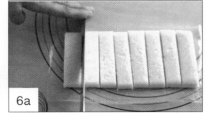

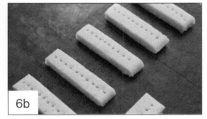

Polka Dot Cookies

These cookies are a playful take on traditional chocolate cookies. I've cut slits into each cookie so that it can sit on the rim of a cup of tea or coffee.

Plain dough

55 g unsalted butter, cut into cubes and chilled

40 g icing sugar

A pinch of salt

90 g cake flour

10 g almond powder extra fine

½ egg yolk (10 g), at room temperature

Cocoa dough

55 g unsalted butter, cut into cubes and chilled

40 g icing sugar

A pinch of salt

80 g cake flour

10 g almond powder extra fine

10 g cocoa powder

½ egg yolk (10 g), at room temperature

1. Place all ingredients for plain dough except egg yolk into a clean resealable plastic bag. Seal bag and shake vigorously to mix ingredients. Freeze for 1 hour. Prepare cocoa dough the same way.

2. Place chilled plain dough mixture in a food processor and pulse until clumpy. Add egg and pulse to form a pliable dough. Wrap in cling film and refrigerate for 30 minutes. Prepare cocoa dough the same way.

3. Preheat oven to 170°C. Line a few baking trays.

4. Transfer plain dough to a work surface covered with cling film and roll into a 3- to 5-mm thick sheet. Prepare cocoa dough the same way.

5. Use a small round piping tip to cut out circles from the plain dough. Repeat to cut out the same number of circles in the cocoa dough.

6. Place the cocoa dough circles into the plain dough, and the plain dough circles into the cocoa dough.

7. Use cookie cutters of your choice to cut shapes from each dough. Use a knife to cut a slit in each shape.

8. Arrange on prepared baking trays. Bake for 13–15 minutes until a little golden around the edges.

9. Leave to cool on a wire rack.

> **TIP**
> The dough becomes a little tricky to work with when it is soft.
> Chill it for a few minutes until it is easy to handle.

Rum Raisin Cookies

These are cookies with a little kick of rum and the sweetness of sun-dried raisins.

Makes about 30 cookies

30 g apricot jam

45 g unsalted butter, at room temperature

45 g caster sugar (extra fine)

A pinch of salt

1/2 egg (30 g)

1 tsp dark rum

54 g cake flour, sifted

Rum-soaked raisins

30–40 g raisins (uncoated)

Dark rum for soaking

Rum icing

40 g icing sugar

1 tsp water

1 tsp dark rum

1. Prepare rum-soaked raisins 2–3 days ahead. Place raisins in a jar or lidded container and add enough rum to cover raisins. Seal with lid and leave raisins to soak for 2–3 days. Drain raisins before using.

2. Preheat oven to 180°C. Line a baking tray. Fit a round piping tip into a piping bag.

3. In a saucepan, heat apricot jam over medium heat, stirring continuously to prevent burning, until jam thickens. Remove from heat and set aside.

4. In a bowl, place butter and beat lightly with a whisk. Add sugar and salt, then whisk to combine.

5. In another bowl, beat egg and rum together. Add egg mixture to butter mixture and mix well. Add flour and stir lightly to incorporate.

6. Transfer to prepared piping bag and pipe 3-cm wide circles on baking tray.

7. Place 3 rum-soaked raisins on each circle. Bake for 13–15 minutes.

8. Remove from oven and brush with thickened apricot jam. Leave to cool.

9. Prepare rum icing. In a bowl, whisk icing sugar and rum to combine. Gradually add water and whisk until sugar is dissolved.

10. Once jam has set, brush a thin coat of rum icing on cookies. Transfer cookies from baking tray onto a wire rack before rum icing hardens.

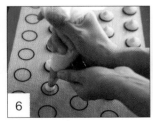

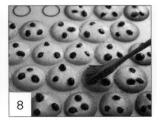

Meringue Pretzels

These dainty cookies, at once savoury and sweet, are a visual delight.

Makes about 40 small cookies

A few drops of food colouring gel (lemon yellow and brown)

40—45 mini pretzels

1¹⁄₂ egg whites (60 g), at room temperature

85 g caster sugar (extra fine)

¹⁄₄ tsp lemon juice or white vinegar

1. Preheat oven to 90°C. Use skewers to colour the inside of a piping bag fitted with a 14-mm round tip. I use the icing gel colours by Wilton.

2. Line a baking tray and arrange pretzels on tray.

3. In a clean heatproof bowl, beat egg white and sugar until combined. Set mixture over a pot of simmering water. Whisk continuously while heating mixture to 55°C.

4. Remove mixture from heat and add lemon juice. Using an electric mixer with a whisk attachment, whisk on high speed until firm peaks form.

5. Adjust speed to low and lightly whisk until meringue is smooth.

6. Transfer to prepared piping bag. Pipe meringue onto pretzels.

7. Bake for 2 hours. Leave in oven for 30—45 minutes to cool completely.

> **TIP**
> Older egg whites are best for making meringues.
> Be careful not to overbeat the egg whites.

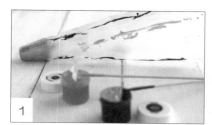

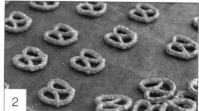

Raisin Cream Cookies

Commonly found in Japan, these cookie sandwiches are rich and luxurious.

110 g cake flour

2 g baking powder

60 g unsalted butter, at room temperature

40 g icing sugar

¹/₂ egg (25 g), at room temperature

25 g almond powder (extra fine)

Rum-soaked raisins

8 tsp water

20 g caster sugar

40 g raisins (uncoated)

2 tsp dark rum

White chocolate buttercream

50 g white baking chocolate

30 g caster sugar

2 tsp water

¹/₂ egg white (24 g)

70 g unsalted butter, at room temperature

1 Prepare rum-soaked raisins a day ahead. In a saucepan, combine water and sugar over medium heat and bring to a boil.

2 Add raisins and continue heating mixture until it starts to boil again. Remove from heat and stir in rum. Transfer to a lidded container. Seal with lid and leave raisins to soak for 24 hours.

3 Sift flour and baking powder together. Set aside.

4 In a bowl, beat butter lightly. Add sugar and whisk until pale. Add egg and mix well before stirring in almond powder.

5 Using a spatula, gently fold in flour until just incorporated and a dough forms. Transfer dough to a work surface covered with cling film and shape into a block. Wrap in cling film and refrigerate for 1 hour.

6 On a work surface covered with cling film, roll chilled dough into a 4-mm thick sheet. Freeze for 15 minutes.

7 Preheat oven to 170°C. Line a baking tray. Fit a piping tip of your choice into a piping bag.

8 Using a 5-cm fluted cookie cutter, or a cookie cutter of your choice, cut shapes from the dough and arrange on prepared baking tray.

9 Bake for 15 minutes. Transfer onto a wire rack to cool.

10 Prepare white chocolate buttercream. Melt chocolate in a heatproof bowl set over a pot of simmering water. Set aside to cool.

11 Follow step 10 on page 81 to make Italian meringue with sugar, water and egg white. Leave to cool.

12 Using an electric mixer with a whisk attachment, whisk butter on medium speed until pale and fluffy. Add meringue in portions and whisk to incorporate after each addition. Add melted chocolate and lightly whisk to combine. Transfer buttercream to prepared piping bag.

13 To assemble, strain raisins and reserve syrup. Brush syrup on the bottom of each cookie. Pipe some buttercream onto a cookie. Spoon some raisins on top before piping more buttercream over. Cover with an unadorned cookie. Repeat to make 10 cookie sandwiches.

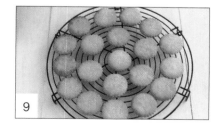

9

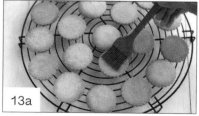

13a

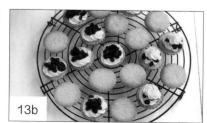

13b

WAFU — A TASTE OF MY HOME

Amazake Dorayaki

A popular Japanese sweet made with traditional ingredients. Make sure that the baking soda you're using is still fresh, as it plays an important role in ensuring the pancake rises and has a fluffy texture.

75 g cake flour

18 g bread flour

2.5 g baking soda

1 1/2 eggs (100 g)

80 g light brown sugar

80 ml *amazake* (non-alcoholic), blended until smooth

225 g sweetened red bean paste

Gyuhi

40 g *shiratamako* (refined glutinous rice flour)

80 ml water

65 g sugar

Cornstarch or potato starch for dusting

1 Sift both flours and baking soda together. Set aside.

2 In a bowl, whisk eggs and sugar until mixture thickens. Add 2 Tbsp *amazake* and stir to combine.

3 Add flour mixture, ensuring that it covers the entire surface of the egg mixture. Using a spatula, lightly fold in flour mixture before mixing in another 2 Tbsp *amazake*.

4 Cover bowl with cling film and set aside at room temperature for 45 minutes to let it thicken. When you scoop up some thickened batter with a spatula, it should drip back into the bowl and be reabsorbed easily. If batter is too thick, adjust consistency with the remaining *amazake*.

5 Heat a non-stick frying pan over medium heat. Use an oil-soaked paper towel to grease frying pan.

6 Test heat by adding a teaspoonful of batter and frying for 45 seconds. When pancake is slightly risen and bubbles appear on its surface, flip to cook the other side for 20 seconds. If the pancake doesn't rise while cooking, add some water to thin the remaining batter slightly.

7 To make 1 pancake, pour a tablespoonful of batter on the pan. Cook for 1 minute, then flip to cook the other side for 20 seconds. Set aside to cool. Repeat to use up batter.

8 Prepare *gyuhi*. Place *shiratamako* in a bowl. Gradually add water, stirring constantly to mix well. Add sugar and mix to combine.

9 Cover bowl loosely with cling film and microwave for 2 minutes. Stir mixture with a damp wooden spoon before microwaving for another minute. Give mixture another stir. At this point it should be translucent.

10 Spread cornstarch on a baking tray and transfer *gyuhi* to tray. Sprinkle with more cornstarch and spread *gyuhi* evenly on tray. Cut *gyuhi* to about 2/3 the size of a pancake or as preferred.

11 To assemble, spread red bean paste on a pancake and place a piece of *gyuhi* on top. Cover with more red bean paste, then top with another pancake. Repeat to use up pancakes. To help *dorayaki* keep their shape, wrap in cling film after assembling.

Ganduki

Brown Sugar Sesame Steamed Cake

This is a famous steamed cake
from the Iwate prefecture.

Makes a 15-cm round cake

150 g cake flour

10 g baking soda

1 egg (50 g)

120 g brown sugar or
  muscovado sugar

21 g honey

5 g white sesame oil

½ tsp light soy sauce

90 ml milk

8 tsp rice vinegar

5 g black sesame seeds,
  roasted

20 g walnuts, roasted
  and chopped

1 Line a 15-cm cake tin. Prepare a steamer and wrap its lid with a tea towel.

2 Sift flour and baking soda together. Set aside.

3 In a bowl, beat egg well. Gradually add sugar and mix until sugar is dissolved.

4 Add honey, oil, soy sauce and milk, mixing well after each addition

5 Sift flour mixture into batter and whisk well.

6 Add vinegar and fold in lightly using a spatula.

7 Pour batter into prepared cake tin and sprinkle with sesame seeds and walnuts.

8 Steam for 10 minutes on high heat, followed by 15 minutes on medium heat.

TIP
If your sugar is lumpy or hard, break up the lumps before
adding it to the egg. You can also make these in small muffin cups,
but monitor and adjust the cooking time accordingly.

Hojicha Daifuku

Roasted Tea Glutinous Rice Cake

Having a cream filling provides a contrasting texture to the mochi skin. *Hojicha* (roasted green tea) balances the sweetness of the red bean paste and cream.

90 g *shiratamako* (refined glutinous rice flour)

45 g caster sugar

5 g *hojicha* powder + more for dusting

160 ml water

Potato starch for dusting

Filling

50 g whipping cream

4 g caster sugar

150 g sweetened red bean paste

1 Prepare filling 1–2 days ahead. Line a baking tray with cling film.

2 Using an electric mixer with a whisk attachment, whisk whipping cream and sugar on high speed until thick and stiff. Transfer to a piping bag and pipe 6 domes onto prepared baking tray. Freeze for a few hours until firm enough to handle.

3 Divide red bean paste into 6 equal portions and shape into balls. Place on a baking tray and refrigerate for at least a few hours, preferably overnight.

4 Flatten a red bean paste ball into a disc and wrap it around a frozen cream dome. Repeat to wrap the other cream domes and refrigerate for at least 2 hours, preferably overnight.

5 Combine *shiratamako*, sugar and *hojicha* powder in a microwave-safe bowl. Add water, stirring until everything is dissolved.

6 Cover bowl loosely with cling film, and microwave at 600W for 2 minutes. Knead mixture lightly using a spatula before microwaving for another minute. At this point mixture should be translucent.

7 Spread potato starch on a baking tray and transfer mochi dough to tray. Sprinkle with more potato starch and flatten dough evenly.

8 Cut mochi dough into 6 equal portions and leave to cool.

9 Place one portion of filling in the middle of a piece of dough. Wrap dough gently around filling, pinching to seal dough. Dust with *hojicha* powder.

TIP
Monitor the texture of the mochi closely while preparing it. Be careful when kneading the mochi dough as it can get very hot.

Mitarashi Dango and Panda Dango

Sweet Soy Sauce Dumplings and Panda Red Bean Dumplings

This is a two-in-one recipe: you get savoury dumplings and sweet ones.
They are also incredibly fun to make.

Makes 9 sticks

Dango dough

120 g *shiratamako* (refined glutinous rice flour)

60 g *joushinko* (fine non-glutinous rice flour)

10 g caster sugar

120 g silken tofu

8–9 tsp water

Vegetable oil for frying

Sweet soy sauce

50 ml water

20 g light brown sugar

1 Tbsp light soy sauce

4 g potato starch

1½ tsp water

Panda dango

60 g sweetened red bean paste

3 g charcoal powder

Water to make charcoal paste

1   Prepare *dango* dough. Combine *shiratamako*, *joushinko* and sugar in a bowl. Add silken tofu and mix well. Gradually add water and knead to get a dough with that has the same firmness as your earlobe.

2   Divide *dango* dough into 2 equal portions and set aside 1 portion for making panda *dango*. Divide the other portion equally into 12 and roll each portion into a ball.

3   Bring a pot of water to a boil. Add balls to boiling water and cook until they float, about 3–5 minutes. Boil for a further 1–2 minutes, then remove from heat and place immediately in a bowl of iced water.

4   Dampen 4 skewers and thread 3 balls onto each skewer. Lightly oil a large skillet and heat over medium heat. Lay *dango* in skillet and cook until lightly browned all over. Rotate skewers for even browning. Set aside.

5   Prepare sweet soy sauce. In a small saucepan, combine all ingredients for sweet soy sauce over medium-low heat. Cook until sauce is clear and thickened. Dip skewered *dango* in sauce to make *mitarashi dango*.

6   Prepare panda *dango*. Shape red bean paste into 5 balls that are 5 g each and 5 balls that are 7 g each.

7   Set aside 45 g of plain *dango* dough. Add a small amount of water to charcoal powder to make a paste. Add charcoal paste to the 45-g portion and knead into dough evenly. Wrap charcoal dough in cling film.

8   Divide the remaining plain dough into 5 equal portions. Divide each portion into a 10-g ball and a 15-g ball. To make a panda head, flatten a 10-g dough ball into a disc and wrap around a 5-g red bean ball. To make a panda body, flatten a 15-g dough ball into a disc and wrap around a 7-g red bean ball. Repeat to make 5 sets. Set aside.

9   Divide charcoal dough into 5 equal portions. Take ³/₄ of each portion to mould into panda legs. Use ²/₃ of the remaining portion to mould into panda ears. Mould the remaining portion into panda eyes, nose and tail. Repeat to make 5 sets of panda features.

10 Cook dough following step 3. Assemble each panda while *dango* is still moist. Thread through dampened skewers and leave to dry.

1a

1b

4

5

9

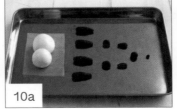

10a

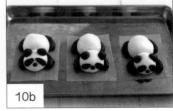

10b

The Halloween
Purple Sweet Potato and Pumpkin Mont Blanc Tart

This tart is a seasonal treat using natural ingredients to produce the fun purple and orange colours associated with Halloween.

Makes an 18-cm tart

80 g whipping cream

8 g caster sugar (extra fine)

Icing sugar for dusting

Tart shell

60 g unsalted butter, cut into cubes and chilled

37 g icing sugar

15 g almond powder (extra fine)

$^1/_3$ egg (20 g)

110 g cake flour

Almond cream

45 g unsalted butter, at room temperature

45 g caster sugar (extra fine)

$^3/_4$ egg (45 g)

45 g almond powder (extra fine)

8 g cornstarch

10 g custard powder

Pumpkin custard cream

100 g pumpkin, peeled and seeds removed

36 g caster sugar (extra fine)

1 egg yolk (20 g)

9 g cake flour, sifted

90 ml milk

1 Prepare almond cream. Follow steps 1–3 to make almond cream (see page 21).

2 Prepare tart shell. Follow steps 1–8 to make basic tart shell (see page 20). Use almond cream as tart filling. Leave to cool completely.

3 Using an electric mixer with a whisk attachment, whisk whipping cream and caster sugar on high speed until stiff peaks form. Transfer to a piping bag and pipe into centre of tart. Using a spatula, shape cream into a cone-like shape, leaving a border between cream and tart edge. Refrigerate until needed.

4 Prepare pumpkin custard cream. Cut pumpkin into cubes and place in a bowl. Steam or microwave until softened, then mash pumpkin until smooth. Add sugar, followed by egg yolk and flour, mixing well after each addition.

5 In a small saucepan, heat milk until just before it boils. Add pumpkin mixture to milk, whisking constantly to incorporate. Cook mixture over medium heat until bubbles start to form in the centre. Remove from heat and place in a baking pan filled with iced water to cool pumpkin custard cream mixture completely.

6 Whisk cooled pumpkin custard cream lightly before transferring to a piping bag. Pipe pumpkin custard cream onto centre of tart, moving the tip in circles to let cream spread evenly. Leave a border between cream and tart edge. Refrigerate until needed.

Purple sweet potato cream

200 g purple sweet potato, peeled

30 g caster sugar (extra fine)

2 Tbsp milk

2 tsp rum

56 g whipping cream

Black cocoa cookies

26 g cake flour

15 g icing sugar

4 g black cocoa powder

5 g cocoa powder

15 g white sesame oil

12 g egg

7 Prepare purple sweet potato cream. Steam or microwave sweet potatoes until softened, then mash until smooth. Add sugar, milk and rum, mixing well after each addition. Push mixture through a fine strainer and set aside.

8 Using an electric mixer with a whisk attachment, whisk whipping cream on high speed until soft peaks form. Add to sweet potato mixture and fold in gently. Transfer to a piping bag fitted with a Mont Blanc tip.

9 Pipe sweet potato cream to make spirals from the edge towards the centre, covering pumpkin custard cream. Dust edge of tart with icing sugar.

10 Prepare black cocoa cookies. Preheat oven to 150°C. Line a baking tray.

11 Place flour, sugar and both cocoa powders in a bowl and mix well. Add oil and egg, then mix lightly using a spatula until a pliable dough forms. Refrigerate dough for 15 minutes.

12 On a lightly floured surface, roll dough into a 3-mm thick sheet. Cut out bat shapes using a bat-shaped cookie cutter, then arrange on prepared baking tray.

13 Bake for 12 minutes. Remove from oven and leave to cool completely. Decorate tart with cookies as desired.

Wa Mont Blanc

Japanese-style Mont Blanc Tartlets

A Japanese take on a classic French dessert, this is a popular dessert among my friends.

5 candied chestnuts

Rum for brushing

60 g chestnut paste

Sweetened red beans for decorating

Icing sugar for dusting

Matcha tart shell

60 g unsalted butter, cut into cubes and chilled

37 g icing sugar

15 g almond powder (extra fine)

$1/3$ egg (20 g)

105 g cake flour

5 g matcha

Almond cream

35 g unsalted butter, at room temperature

35 g caster sugar (extra fine)

$1/2$ egg (35 g)

35 g almond powder (extra fine)

6 g cornstarch

5 g custard powder

Red bean cream

85 g whipping cream

55 g sweetened red bean paste

Chestnut cream

63 g whipping cream

160 g chestnut paste

18 g unsalted butter, at room temperature

1 tsp rum

1 Prepare almond cream. Follow steps 1–3 to make almond cream (see page 21).

2 Prepare matcha tart shell. Follow steps 1–5 to make basic tart shell (see page 20). Sift matcha and add to cake flour before combining with batter.

3 Prepare six 6.5-cm tart tins. Use an 8-cm mousse ring to cut 6 circles from rolled out dough. Drape each dough circle over a tart tin and gently press it in. Trim edges and poke holes in tart shells using a fork. Pipe almond cream to fill tarts.

4 Roughly chop 3 candied chestnuts, divide into 6 equal portions and spoon over almond cream. Refrigerate tarts while preheating oven.

5 Preheat oven to 170°C.

6 Bake for 30 minutes. Remove from oven and unmould onto a wire rack. Brush tarts all over with rum while they are still hot. Leave to cool completely.

7 Divide 60 g chestnut paste into 6 equal portions and shape into balls. Set aside.

8 Prepare red bean cream. Using an electric mixer with a whisk attachment, whisk whipping cream on high speed until stiff peaks form. Fold in red bean paste, then transfer to a piping bag.

9 Pipe a layer of red bean cream on each tart, then top with a chestnut paste ball. Pipe more cream to cover chestnut paste ball. Using a spatula, shape cream into a cone-like shape. Refrigerate for 30 minutes.

10 Prepare chestnut cream. Using an electric mixer with a whisk attachment, whisk whipping cream on medium speed until soft peaks form. Set aside 20 g for decoration.

11 In another bowl, use a spatula to stir chestnut paste until smooth, then mix in butter. Add rum and the remaining whipping cream, then mix well. Transfer to a piping bag fitted with a Mont Blanc tip.

12 Pipe chestnut cream to make spirals from the bottom to the top, covering red bean cream.

13 To decorate Mont Blanc tartlets, spoon reserved whipping cream on top. Chop the remaining candied chestnuts into small pieces. Arrange chestnut pieces and red beans on tarts, then dust with icing sugar.

Kinako and Black Sesame Dacquoise

This almond meringue cookie sandwich is sure to be a hit at a tea party.

Makes 9 cookie sandwiches

3 egg whites (110 g)

70 g almond powder
(extra fine)

55 g icing sugar

15 g cake flour

7 g *kinako* (roasted
soybean flour)

A pinch of salt

40 g caster sugar
(extra fine)

Blueberry jam for filling

Black sesame buttercream

70 g unsalted butter, at
room temperature

$^1/_2$ egg white (20 g)

30 g caster sugar
(extra fine)

2 tsp water

10 g black sesame
paste

1. Preheat oven to 170°C. Line a baking tray. Place a 1-mm thick chablon (silicone stencil mat) with 7 x 4.5-cm oblong moulds on top. Prepare a piping bag.

2. Keep egg whites in freezer while measuring the rest of the ingredients.

3. Sift almond powder, icing sugar, flour and *kinako* together twice. Set aside.

4. Using an electric mixer with a whisk attachment, whisk egg whites and salt on high speed until firm peaks form. Gradually add caster sugar and whisk until stiff peaks form.

5. Add almond powder mixture to meringue and fold in using a spatula until just combined. Transfer to prepared piping bag.

6. Pipe batter into moulds. Using a small palette knife, carefully scrape off any excess batter to ensure clean edges. Gently remove chablon.

7. Sprinkle with icing sugar and leave to absorb into batter until no longer visible before sprinkling with icing sugar again.

8. Bake for 12–14 minutes. Transfer dacquoise onto a wire rack immediately and leave to cool.

9. Prepare black sesame buttercream. Cut butter into small cubes and set aside. Fit a star piping tip into a piping bag.

10. Using an electric mixer with a whisk attachment, whisk egg white on high speed until firm peaks form. Place sugar and water in a microwave-safe bowl and microwave at 500W for 90 seconds to make a syrup. Gradually add syrup to egg white, keeping the electric mixer on high speed. Whisk until meringue reaches 45°C and is glossy.

11. In another bowl, whisk butter on medium speed until fluffy. Add meringue and whisk to combine before mixing in black sesame paste. Transfer to prepared piping bag.

12. Pipe a ring of buttercream around the edge of a dacquoise cookie. Fill its centre with blueberry jam. Cover with an unadorned cookie. Repeat to make 9 cookie sandwiches.

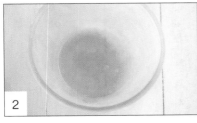

2

4

5

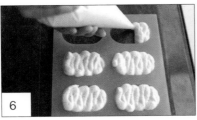

6

8

12

Zen

Matcha and Black Sesame Panna Cotta

The arrowroot gives this pudding a unique and delightful texture.

Makes 5 servings

**Black sesame
panna cotta**

13 g arrowroot flour

26 g caster sugar
(extra fine)

87 ml water

87 ml milk

15 g black sesame
paste

Matcha panna cotta

11 g matcha

4 tsp hot water,
combined with 12 g
caster sugar

40 g arrowroot flour

55 g caster sugar
(extra fine)

262 ml milk

262 ml water

1 Prepare black sesame panna cotta. Prepare five 125-ml pudding cups. Fill a baking pan with iced water.

2 In a saucepan, combine flour, sugar and $^1/_3$ of water. Stir to dissolve flour and sugar, then add milk and the remaining water.

3 Heat flour mixture over medium heat while stirring constantly until mixture is sticky. Continue stirring and heat for another 7–10 minutes until mixture thickens.

4 Add black sesame paste, mix well and bring mixture to a boil.

5 Divide black sesame mixture equally into prepared pudding cups. Place pudding cups in prepared baking pan to chill and set.

6 Prepare matcha panna cotta. Place matcha and hot water mixture in a small bowl, then whisk until matcha is dissolved.

7 Follow steps 2–4 to prepare matcha panna cotta. Add matcha mixture in place of black sesame paste.

8 Slowly pour matcha mixture over black sesame panna cotta, dividing it equally into the 5 pudding cups.

9 Cover with cling film, ensuring that the cling film adheres to the surface of the matcha mixture.

10 Place pudding cups in baking pan to chill and set before refrigerating for 1–2 days.

11 Gently press around edges of panna cotta before inverting each pudding cup onto a plate to unmould.

TIP
You can use a digital scale to measure liquids like water
and milk, when 1 gram = 1 millilitre.

Matcha Tiramisu

Matcha is a great flavour swap for coffee and cocoa in tiramisu. It has such a lovely colour as well.

Makes a 15-cm square cake

80 g sweetened red
bean paste

Matcha for dusting

Matcha genoise sponge

6 g matcha, sifted

62 g cake flour

12 g unsalted butter

3½ tsp milk

2 eggs (130 g)

65 g caster sugar
(extra fine)

15 g glucose

Matcha syrup

30 g caster sugar
(extra fine)

2 g matcha

60 ml hot water

Mascarpone mousse

180 g whipping cream

40 g condensed milk

180 g mascarpone
cheese

1 Prepare matcha syrup. Place sugar in a bowl and sift in matcha. Add hot water and whisk until sugar and matcha are dissolved. Set aside.

2 Prepare matcha genoise sponge. Sift matcha and flour together twice.

3 Follow steps 1–8 to prepare matcha genoise sponge (see page 19). Use a 15-cm square cake tin and bake for 20–25 minutes.

4 Invert onto a wire rack and leave in cake tin for a few minutes. Unmould, flip cake over and cover with a damp tea towel. Leave to cool completely. Slice cooled cake into halves horizontally. Set aside.

5 Prepare mascarpone mousse. Using an electric mixer with a whisk attachment, whisk whipping cream and condensed milk on high speed until soft peaks form. Refrigerate until needed.

6 In another bowl, whisk mascarpone cheese lightly. Add ½ of whipping cream mixture and whisk to combine. Add this mixture to the remaining whipping cream mixture and fold in using a spatula.

7 To assemble, tightly wrap the bottom of a 15-cm square cake ring with cling film, then place on a cake board or stand.

8 Place 1 layer of cake inside cake ring and brush with matcha syrup. Spread ¼ of mascarpone mousse evenly on top, followed by red bean paste. Cover evenly with another ¼ of mascarpone mousse.

9 Place next layer of cake on top and brush with matcha syrup. Add the remaining mascarpone mousse and spread evenly, making the surface as smooth as possible. Refrigerate for 1–2 hours.

10 Remove square cake ring and cut into 6 equal portions. Use a sift to dust matcha on top.

CROWD-PLEASING SPONGE AND ROLL CAKES

Hojicha and Coffee Sponge Cake

As both *hojicha* and coffee are roasted,
they are flavours that go together nicely.

Makes a 16-cm round cake

3 egg whites (120 g)

7 g *hojicha* powder

40 g cake flour

3 egg yolks (60 g)

35 g light brown sugar

25 g white sesame oil

4 tsp milk

3 egg whites (120 g)

$^1/_2$ tsp lemon juice or
  white vinegar

40 g caster sugar
  (extra fine)

Coffee cream

4 g instant coffee
  granules

4 tsp hot water

285 g whipping cream

32 g caster sugar
  (extra fine)

1 Preheat oven at 180°C. Line a 28-cm square cake tin.

2 Keep egg whites in freezer while measuring the rest of the ingredients. Sift *hojicha* powder and flour together twice. Set aside.

3 Using an electric mixer with a whisk attachment, whisk egg yolks and light brown sugar on high speed until mixture reaches the ribbon stage. When you lift the whisk, the batter should fall slowly and form ribbons that hold their shape.

4 Gradually add oil and whisk until emulsified. Add milk and mix well. Add flour mixture to egg yolk mixture and whisk to incorporate.

5 In a clean bowl, whisk egg whites and lemon juice on high speed. Gradually add caster sugar, whisking continuously until firm peaks form.

6 Fold $^1/_3$ of meringue into batter. When a few white streaks are still visible, add another $^1/_3$ of meringue and fold in.

7 Add batter to the remaining meringue and stir lightly to combine.

8 Pour batter into prepared cake tin and spread evenly. Tap cake tin lightly against a hard surface to release any bubbles. Bake for 10–12 minutes.

9 Remove onto a wire rack, cover with cling film and leave to cool. Cut cooled cake crosswise into 5 equal strips, about 6-cm wide.

10 Prepare coffee cream. Add instant coffee granules to hot water, stirring until they are dissolved. Leave to cool completely.

11 Using an electric mixer with a whisk attachment, whisk whipping cream and sugar on high speed until firm peaks form. Divide into 2 equal portions and refrigerate until needed.

12 Add $^1/_2$ of coffee to 1 portion of whipping cream and mix using a spatula. Spread a thin layer of coffee cream evenly on each cake strip.

13 Roll up a cake strip from its short edge. Place the first roll on the short edge of another cake strip and roll up the second cake strip around the first roll. Repeat with the next 3 cake strips to form a large round cake. Wrap large roll cake in cling film and refrigerate for 30 minutes.

14 Combine the remaining coffee and whipping cream, mixing well using a spatula. Cover top and sides of cake with coffee cream and smooth it out with a bench scraper and offset spatula. Use any remaining cream to decorate cake as desired.

TIP
As the coffee cream separates easily, it's better to combine the coffee and cream just before using it.

Mandarin Orange Biscuit Roll

This roll is bursting with the sweetness of mandarin oranges and is very refreshing.

150 g whipping cream

12 g caster sugar (extra fine)

1 tsp orange liqueur

8–10 mandarin oranges, peeled

Biscuit sponge

2¹⁄₂ egg yolks (50 g)

65 g caster sugar (extra fine)

2¹⁄₂ egg whites (100 g)

60 g cake flour

1. Preheat oven to 185°C. Prepare a 28-cm square sheet of baking paper and place on the back of a square cake tin.
2. Prepare biscuit sponge. Beat egg yolks and 15 g sugar until mixture becomes pale.
3. In a separate clean bowl, whisk egg whites and the remaining sugar until soft peaks form.
4. Add ¹⁄₃ of meringue into egg yolk mixture and mix gently using a whisk. Add the remaining meringue and fold in lightly using a spatula.
5. Sift flour into batter and fold to incorporate.
6. Transfer batter to a piping bag fitted with a 14-mm round tip. Pipe batter diagonally on prepared baking paper.
7. Bake for 10 minutes.
8. Remove from oven. Cover top of biscuit sponge with a sheet of baking paper before covering with cling film. Leave on cake tin to cool completely.
9. Using an electric mixer, whisk whipping cream and sugar on high speed until firm peaks form. Mix in orange liqueur, then transfer to a piping bag fitted with a flat tip.
10. Measure the circumference of an orange. Trim biscuit sponge so that its width is 5 cm longer than the orange's circumference.
11. Pipe whipping cream in straight lines to cover biscuit sponge. Lay oranges on their sides in a row in the centre. Lift opposite edges of biscuit sponge to cover the oranges and meet at the top. Press edges together.
12. Wrap roll cake in baking paper, followed by cling film. Refrigerate for 3 hours before unwrapping to serve.

Snow Roll

This is a very pale sponge filled with a light ruby chocolate cream. If your sponge is beginning to brown in the oven, remove to cover the cake tin with foil before returning it to the oven.

30 g white sesame oil

10 g condensed milk

65 ml milk

70 g cake flour, sifted

70 g caster sugar
(extra fine)

5 egg whites (200 g)

1 g egg white powder

Chocolate cream

60 g ruby chocolate

180 g whipping cream

1 Prepare chocolate cream a day ahead. Place ruby chocolate in a bowl.

2 In a small saucepan, heat whipping cream until just before it boils. Remove from heat and gradually pour over chocolate, whisking continuously until emulsified.

3 Place in a baking pan filled with iced water. When chocolate cream is cooled, cover with cling film, ensuring that the cling film adheres to the surface of the cream. Refrigerate overnight.

4 Prepare sponge cake. Preheat oven to 160°C. Line a 28-cm square cake tin with reusable baking paper.

5 In a microwave-safe bowl, mix oil, condensed milk and milk. Microwave until mixture is 45°C.

6 While oil mixture is warm, sift in flour. Mix well and set aside.

7 In another bowl, combine 1 Tbsp sugar, egg whites and egg white powder. Using an electric mixer with a whisk attachment, whisk until foamy. Gradually add the remaining sugar and whisk until soft peaks form.

8 Add $1/3$ of meringue to flour mixture and mix well. Fold in the remaining meringue in 2 equal portions.

9 Pour batter into prepared cake tin and spread evenly.

10 Bake for 14—16 minutes. Place a sheet of baking paper on a wire rack and invert cake onto it. Unmould cake, peel off baking paper halfway and leave to cool completely.

11 To assemble, remove baking paper completely. Bevel 1 end of the cake by slicing off a 1-cm wide portion at an angle.

12 Whisk chocolate cream lightly then spread evenly on cake, leaving bevelled edge uncoated. From the opposite edge, roll up cake to form a log. Refrigerate for 3 hours before serving chilled.

San Sebastian

A chequerboard cake, this is named after the famous cobblestoned streets in the Basque region of Spain.

Makes a 15-cm round cake

4 eggs (240 g)

160 g caster sugar
(extra fine)

100 g apricot jam, warmed

Plain sponge mix

30 g unsalted butter

2 tsp milk

80 g cake flour, sifted

Cocoa sponge mix

30 g unsalted butter

2 tsp milk

10 g cocoa powder

70 g cake flour, sifted

Earl Grey ganache

100 g whipping cream

5 g Earl Grey tea leaves

3–4 tsp milk

20 g glucose

100 g baking chocolate,
roughly chopped

1 Preheat oven to 170°C. Line two 15-cm round cake tins. Cut out a 3.5-cm circle, 7.5-cm circle and 11-cm circle from baking paper as guides.

2 Place eggs and sugar in a heatproof bowl set over a pot of simmering water. Whisking continuously, heat mixture until it reaches 40°C.

3 Using an electric mixer with a whisk attachment, whisk egg mixture on high speed until mixture reaches the ribbon stage. When you lift the whisk, the batter should fall slowly and form ribbons that hold their shape. Adjust speed to low and whisk for 2 minutes. Divide equally into 2 bowls. Lightly whisk each portion until smooth.

4 Prepare plain sponge mix. Place butter and milk in a heatproof bowl set over a pot of simmering water. Heat until combined. Set aside in a pan filled with warm water.

5 Add flour in 3 equal portions to one bowl of batter, folding to incorporate after each addition. Add a scoop of batter to the melted butter mixture and mix well. Pour mixture into batter and fold in lightly.

6 Transfer plain sponge batter to a prepared cake tin. Using a skewer, stir batter in cake tin to release any bubbles.

7 Follow steps 4–6 to prepare cocoa sponge batter. Sift cocoa powder into melted butter mixture before adding a scoop of batter to it.

8 Bake for 25–30 minutes. Remove from oven and drop cake tin onto a hard surface to release excess steam. Invert onto a wire rack and leave to cool in cake tin for 2–3 minutes. Unmould, flip cake over and cover with a damp tea towel. Leave to cool completely.

9 Cut cooled cakes horizontally into 1.5-cm thick slices. Using the prepared paper guides, cut out 3 concentric rings and a 3.5-cm circle from each slice. Start with the largest guide to cut out an 11-cm circle.

10 To assemble, place rings for 1 layer inside one another, alternating the colours. Brush apricot jam on top before assembling the next layer.

11 Prepare Earl Grey ganache. In a saucepan, warm whipping cream over medium heat. Add tea leaves and bring mixture to a boil. Remove from heat and leave to steep for 5 minutes.

12 Strain tea mixture and weigh it. Add enough milk so that mixture is 100 g. Return mixture to saucepan and add glucose. Heat until just before it boils, stirring continuously. Pour over chocolate and mix well. Leave to cool to room temperature.

13 Coat cake with a thin layer of ganache and refrigerate for 5–10 minutes. Once crumb coat is set, pour remaining ganache over cake. If ganache is too thick, reheat by setting it over a pot of boiling water briefly.

9

10

13

Banana Omelette

This is very easy to make, which means it's perfect if you have to host last-minute guests.

2 egg yolks (40 g)

60 g caster sugar
(extra fine)

1¹/₂ egg whites (60 g)

60 g cake flour

4 ripe medium bananas,
sliced

Icing sugar for dusting

Mascarpone cream

80 g whipping cream

20 g condensed milk

1 tsp brandy

80 g mascarpone
cheese

1 Preheat oven to 210°C. Fit a piping bag with a 1-cm round tip and another piping bag with an open star tip. Draw four 12-cm circles to use as guides on a sheet of baking paper, then line a baking tray with it. Cover with another layer of baking paper.

2 Prepare sponge biscuit. Using an electric mixer with a whisk attachment, whisk egg yolks and 30 g caster sugar on high speed until mixture is doubled in volume, thick and fluffy.

3 In a clean bowl, whisk egg whites on high speed until slightly foamy. Add the remaining caster sugar gradually, whisking well after each addition. Keep whisking until stiff peaks form.

4 Add ¹/₃ of meringue into egg yolk mixture and mix gently using a whisk. Add the remaining meringue and fold in lightly using a spatula.

5 Sift flour into batter and fold in until incorporated.

6 Transfer to piping bag fitted with a round tip. Use guides on baking paper to pipe four 12-cm circles onto baking tray. Bake for 6–7 minutes until light brown.

7 Remove from oven and cover with a sheet of baking paper. Invert onto a wire rack and peel off the 2 layers of baking paper. Flip the biscuit sponge circles, cover with a clean sheet of baking paper and leave to cool completely.

8 Prepare mascarpone cream. Using an electric mixer with a whisk attachment, whisk whipping cream, condensed milk and brandy on high speed until soft peaks form. In a separate bowl, whisk mascarpone cheese until softened. Add ¹/₂ of whipping cream mixture and mix well. Add this mixture to the remaining whipping cream mixture and fold in using a spatula. Transfer to piping bag fitted with an open star tip.

9 To assemble, flip a biscuit sponge circle so that its underside is facing up. Pipe a ring of mascarpone cream on top, keeping 1 cm away from the edge. Lay slices of banana in the middle. Fold biscuit sponge circle to sandwich banana and cream. Repeat to make 4 banana omelettes.

10 Dust with icing sugar.

2a

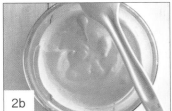
2b

3

4

6

7

9

Komeko Cake

Gluten-free Rice Flour Cake

This cake is gluten-free, fruity and unbelievably light.
Another bonus: there's no sifting required!

1 Tbsp water or soy milk

15 g white sesame oil

A few drops of vanilla extract

2 eggs (120 g)

60 g caster sugar (extra fine)

70 g *komeko* (rice flour)

Mango for decorating, peeled and sliced

Syrup

70 ml water

95 g caster sugar (extra fine)

Mango cream

250 g whipping cream

20 g caster sugar (extra fine)

50 g mango purée, at room temperature

1 Preheat oven to 170°C. Line a 15-cm round cake tin.

2 Prepare syrup. In a covered saucepan, combine water and sugar over medium heat until sugar is dissolved and mixture is clear. Leave to cool.

3 In another bowl, combine water, oil and vanilla extract. Set aside in a pan filled with warm water.

4 Place eggs and sugar in a heatproof bowl set over a pot of simmering water. Heat until mixture is 40°C, then remove from heat.

5 Using an electric mixer with a whisk attachment, whisk egg mixture on high speed until mixture reaches the ribbon stage. When you lift the whisk, the batter should fall slowly and form ribbons that hold their shape. Adjust speed to low and whisk for 2 minutes.

6 Add *komeko* to batter and fold in using a spatula. Add a scoop of batter to the oil mixture and mix well. Add this mixture into the batter and fold until batter looks glossy.

7 Pour batter into prepared cake tin. Tap cake tin a few times against a hard surface to release any bubbles. Bake for 25 minutes.

8 Invert onto a wire rack and leave in cake tin for a few minutes. Unmould, flip cake over and cover with a damp tea towel. Leave to cool completely. Cover with cling film to keep cake moist.

9 Unmould and slice cake into thirds horizontally. Use a heart-shaped ring mould to cut out a heart from each cake layer. If you do not have one, use a heart-shaped template cut out from baking paper as a guide.

10 Prepare mango cream. Using an electric mixer with a whisk attachment, whisk whipping cream, sugar and mango purée on high speed until soft peaks form. Adjust speed to low to prevent over-whisking.

11 Set aside ¹/₂ of mango cream and refrigerate until needed. Continue whisking the remaining mango cream until stiff peaks form.

12 To assemble, brush syrup on a cake layer. Spread a layer of cream evenly before arranging mango slices on top. Add second cake layer on top and repeat with syrup, cream and mango. Top with third cake layer and brush with syrup. Coat entire cake with a thin layer of cream and refrigerate for 30 minutes.

13 Whisk the second portion of mango cream until firm peaks form. Cover top and sides of cake with cream and smooth over with a bench scraper and offset spatula. Decorate with mango slices as desired.

Strawberry Shortcake

This recipe calls for some homemade strawberry purée to be added to the cream. It gives the cream an extra burst of strawberry flavour.

15–20 strawberries, stems removed, hulled and cut lengthwise into halves

Genoise sponge

15 g unsalted butter

1½ Tbsp milk

2½ eggs (140 g)

1 egg yolk (15 g)

75 g caster sugar (extra fine)

20 g glucose

75 g cake flour, sifted

Strawberry purée

450 g fresh or frozen strawberries, stems removed

45 g caster sugar

1 Tbsp lemon juice

Syrup

12 g caster sugar (extra fine)

2 tsp lemon juice

40 g strawberry purée (see above)

Strawberry cream

200 g whipping cream

16 g caster sugar (extra fine)

75 g strawberry purée (see above)

Frosting

150 g whipping cream

12 g caster sugar (extra fine)

1 Prepare strawberry purée. In a medium saucepan, place strawberries, sugar and lemon juice. Leave to sit for 30 minutes.

2 Heat mixture over medium heat for 10–15 minutes, stirring constantly to mash strawberries into small pieces. Strain purée and leave to cool before refrigerating until needed.

3 Preheat oven to 170°C. Line a 15-cm square cake tin.

4 Follow steps 1–9 to make genoise sponge (see page 19). Bake batter in prepared 15-cm square cake tin. Slice cake into thirds horizontally.

5 Prepare syrup. Place all ingredients for syrup in a bowl and mix until sugar is dissolved.

6 Prepare strawberry cream. Using an electric mixer with a whisk attachment, whisk whipping cream and sugar on medium speed until soft peaks form. Adjust speed to low to prevent over-whisking. Add strawberry purée and fold in using a spatula.

7 To assemble, brush syrup on a cake layer. Spread a layer of cream evenly before adding the second cake layer. Brush with syrup, spread a layer of cream, then arrange strawberries on top. Cover strawberries with more cream. Top with the third cake layer and brush with syrup. Refrigerate until frosting is ready.

8 Prepare frosting. Using an electric mixer with a whisk attachment, whisk whipping cream and sugar on medium speed until firm peaks form. Adjust speed to low to prevent over-whisking. Cover top of cake evenly with frosting and refrigerate for 30 minutes.

9 Trim sides of cake and cut into 4 equal slices. Decorate with any remaining cream as desired.

2

6

7a

7b

7c

9

PRETTY MOUSSE DELIGHTS

Chocolate Lovers

This is a must try for chocoholics! It has a surprising crunchy bite that contrasts well with the creamy and light mousse.

250 g whipping cream

3 g gelatine leaf

65 g milk baking
    chocolate

65 g dark baking
    chocolate

Ganache

50 g ruby baking
    chocolate

45 g whipping cream

Pâté à bombe

1¹/₂ egg yolks 30 g)

4 tsp water

20 g caster sugar
    (extra fine)

1   Prepare 8 oval ice cream moulds and 8 ice cream sticks.

2   Prepare ganache. Place ruby chocolate in a bowl. Heat whipping cream
    in a saucepan over medium heat and bring to a boil. Remove from heat
    and pour over ruby chocolate. Leave to sit for 2–3 minutes before
    mixing to combine. Transfer to a piping bag and refrigerate until needed.

3   Using an electric mixer with a whisk attachment, whisk whipping cream
    on high speed until soft peaks form. Refrigerate until needed.

4   Soak 3 g gelatine in a bowl of iced water for 20 minutes. Drain and
    squeeze to remove excess water. Set aside.

5   Melt milk chocolate in a heatproof bowl set over a pot of simmering
    water. Melt dark chocolate in another heatproof bowl set over a pot of
    simmering water. Set aside.

6   Prepare *pâté à bombe*. Place egg yolks, water and sugar in a heatproof
    bowl set over a pot of simmering water. Whisking continuously, heat
    mixture until it thickens slightly and reaches 80°C.

7   Remove from heat and whisk until pale and fluffy. Add gelatine and
    stir to combine.

8   Fold in ¹/₂ of *pâté à bombe* to melted milk chocolate. Repeat to fold in
    the other ¹/₂ of *pâté à bombe* to melted dark chocolate. Leave to cool
    until room temperature.

9   Add ¹/₂ of chilled whipping cream to milk chocolate mixture and stir to
    combine. Transfer to a piping bag.

10 Pipe milk chocolate mousse equally into prepared ice cream moulds.
    Place an ice cream stick on 1 end of each ice cream mould. The stick
    should sit on top of the mousse. Freeze for 10–15 minutes until mousse
    is slightly hard.

11 Pipe ganache in the centre of each mould, covering the ice cream
    sticks. Refrigerate for 5 minutes.

Cocoa cookies

102 g cake flour

30 g icing sugar

18 g cocoa powder

32 g white sesame oil

$1/2$ egg (25 g)

Mirror glaze

10 g gelatine leaf

125 ml water

225 g caster sugar
(extra fine)

150 g baking chocolate

30 g cocoa powder,
sifted

65 g whipping cream

12 Add the remaining chilled whipping cream to dark chocolate mixture and stir to combine. Transfer to a piping bag.

13 Pipe dark chocolate mousse to cover ganache and fill ice cream moulds completely. Freeze until mousse is set.

14 Prepare cocoa cookies. Preheat oven to 150°C. Line a baking tray.

15 Place flour, sugar and cocoa powder in a bowl. Add oil and egg, then mix lightly using a spatula until a dough forms. Wrap in cling film and refrigerate for 15 minutes.

16 Transfer dough to a work surface covered with cling film and roll into a 3-mm thick sheet. Cut out 8 oval shapes that are the same size as ice cream moulds.

17 Arrange on prepared baking tray and bake for 18 minutes. Remove onto a wire rack and leave to cool.

18 Prepare mirror glaze. Soak gelatine in a bowl of iced water for 20 minutes. Drain and squeeze to remove excess water. Set aside.

19 Place water and sugar in a saucepan and bring to a boil. When mixture reaches 104°C, add chocolate.

20 Stir to combine. Add cocoa powder and mix well, followed by whipping cream.

21 When mixture reaches 60°C, remove from heat, add gelatine and mix well. Strain into a bowl.

22 Blend mixture well using an immersion blender. Strain again into a jar and leave to cool until 35°C.

23 Arranged cooled cookies on a tray. Dip a frozen mousse stick into the cooled mirror glaze to coat. Let excess mirror glaze drip off, then place on top of a cocoa cookie. Repeat to make 8 sticks.

13

17

23a

23b

Summer Verrines

Mango and Passion Fruit Mousse

You will find tropical fruity flavours in this delicate mousse. If you are able to prop up and leave your serving glasses at an angle, you can create some fun designs too.

Makes 6 servings

Mango for garnishing,
peeled and cubed

Mint for garnishing

Cheese mousse

2 g gelatine leaf

100 g whipping cream

4 tsp milk

1 egg yolk (24 g)

15 g caster sugar
(extra fine)

55 g mascarpone
cheese

Mango mousse

3 g gelatine leaf

80 g whipping cream

5 g caster sugar
(extra fine)

100 g mango purée, at
room temperature

20 g passion fruit purée,
at room temperature

Passion fruit jelly

4 g gelatine leaf

12 g caster sugar
(extra fine)

180 ml water

80 g passion fruit purée,
at room temperature

70 g mango purée, at
room temperature

1 Prepare 6 serving glasses.

2 Prepare cheese mousse. Soak gelatine in a bowl of iced water for 20 minutes. Drain and squeeze to remove excess water. Set aside.

3 Using an electric mixer with a whisk attachment, whisk 80 g whipping cream on high speed until soft peaks form. Refrigerate until needed.

4 In a small saucepan, combine milk and the remaining whipping cream over medium heat until just before mixture boils. Remove from heat.

5 In a bowl, place egg yolk and caster sugar. Add 1 Tbsp milk mixture and mix to combine. Stir in the remaining milk mixture.

6 Return mixture to saucepan and heat over low heat until it thickens. Remove from heat and add gelatine. Stir until gelatine is dissolved.

7 Transfer to a clean bowl and gradually add mascarpone cheese, mixing well using a whisk. Leave to cool.

8 Add cooled mascarpone cheese mixture to chilled whipping cream and mix using a spatula. Transfer to a piping bag.

9 Pipe equally into prepared serving glasses. Tap glasses gently against a hard surface to release any bubbles. Refrigerate for 5–15 minutes until mousse is set.

10 Prepare mango mousse. Soak gelatine in a bowl of iced water for 20 minutes. Drain and squeeze to remove excess water. Set aside.

11 Using an electric mixer with a whisk attachment, whisk whipping cream on high speed until soft peaks form. Refrigerate until needed.

12 In a saucepan, combine sugar and both purées over medium heat until mixture is 60°C. Remove from heat, add gelatine and mix well. Refrigerate for about 5 minutes until mixture thickens slightly.

13 Add cooled mango mixture to chilled whipping cream and fold in. Transfer to a piping bag. Pipe equally into serving glasses over cheese mousse. Refrigerate for 5–15 minutes until mousse is set.

14 Prepare passion fruit jelly. Soak gelatine in a bowl of iced water for 20 minutes. Drain and squeeze to remove excess water. Set aside.

15 In a saucepan, combine sugar, water and both purées over medium heat until mixture is 60°C. Remove from heat, add gelatine and mix well. Refrigerate until mixture thickens slightly.

16 Pour into serving glasses over mango mousse. Refrigerate until jelly is set. Decorate with mango and mint as desired.

9

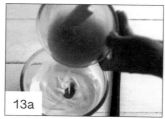
13a

13b

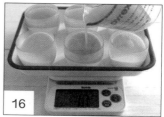
16

Mirror Mousse Cake

This cake is one of my husband's favourites. It is a decadent combination of dark chocolate and raspberries.

3

5

13a

13b

17

18a

18b

13-cm round genoise sponge slice, 1.5-cm thick (see page 19)

Raspberry jelly

2 g gelatine leaf

100 g raspberry purée, at room temperature

15 g caster sugar (extra fine)

Chocolate mousse

45 g whipping cream

35 g baking chocolate (about 50% cocoa solids)

3 Tbsp milk

Raspberry mousse

7 g gelatine leaf

200 g whipping cream

110 g raspberry purée, at room temperature

50 g caster sugar (extra fine)

Mirror glaze

10 g gelatine leaf

125 ml water

225 g caster sugar (extra fine)

150 g baking chocolate

30 g cocoa powder, sifted

65 g whipping cream

1   Prepare cake 1–2 days ahead. Tightly wrap the bottoms of a 9-cm round cake ring, 11-cm round cake ring and 15-cm round cake ring with cling film.

2   Prepare raspberry jelly. Soak gelatine in a bowl of iced water for 20 minutes. Drain and squeeze to remove excess water. Set aside.

3   In a saucepan, combine raspberry purée and sugar over medium heat and bring to a boil. Remove from heat and leave to cool until 60°C before adding gelatine. Stir until gelatine is dissolved.

4   Place 9-cm cake ring on a baking tray and pour in jelly mixture. Refrigerate until jelly is set.

5   Place 11-cm cake ring on a baking tray. Unmould jelly and place in the centre of the cake ring. Set aside.

6   Prepare chocolate mousse. Using an electric mixer with a whisk attachment, whisk whipping cream on medium speed until soft peaks form. Refrigerate until needed.

7   Place chocolate in a bowl. In a small saucepan, heat milk until just before it boils. Pour milk over chocolate and mix well to make a ganache. Leave to cool.

8   Add whipping cream to chocolate ganache and fold in. Transfer chocolate mousse into 11-cm cake ring and freeze for a few hours, preferably overnight, until it sets.

9   Prepare raspberry mousse. Soak gelatine in a bowl of iced water for 20 minutes. Drain and squeeze to remove excess water. Set aside.

10 Using an electric mixer with a whisk attachment, whisk whipping cream on high speed until soft peaks form. Refrigerate until needed.

11 In a saucepan, combine raspberry purée and sugar over medium heat until sugar is dissolved. Remove from heat and leave to cool until 60°C before adding gelatine. Stir until gelatine is dissolved. Place in a baking pan filled with iced water to cool until slightly thickened.

12 Add whipping cream to raspberry mixture and fold in.

13 Place 15-cm cake ring on a baking tray and pour in ¹/₂ of raspberry mousse. Gently place raspberry jelly and chocolate mousse in the centre. Pour over the remaining raspberry mousse, then place the genoise sponge on top. Freeze cake overnight.

14 Prepare mirror glaze. Soak gelatine in a bowl of iced water for 20 minutes. Drain and squeeze to remove excess water. Set aside.

15 Place water and sugar in a saucepan and bring to a boil. When mixture reaches 104°C, add chocolate. Stir to combine.

16 Add cocoa powder and mix well, followed by whipping cream. When mixture reaches 60°C, remove from heat, add gelatine and mix well. Strain into a bowl.

17 Blend mixture well using an immersion blender. Strain again into a jar and leave to cool until 30–35°C.

18 Unmould cake and place on top of a 12-cm round cake tin set in a baking pan. Pour mirror glaze over cake. Using a spatula, scrape excess glaze dripping off the bottom of the cake. Refrigerate cake for 5 minutes to set mirror glaze.

Mocha

Coffee & Caramel Cream Cake

The flavours of coffee and chocolate go so well together. Add caramel, and it's another winning combination.

25 g baking chocolate

Mirror gel for brushing

Joconde sponge

1 egg white (35 g)

18 g caster sugar (extra fine)

$^1/_3$ egg (21 g)

15 g almond powder

15 g icing sugar

13 g cake flour, sifted

1 g instant coffee granules, sifted

Coffee essence

50 g caster sugar (extra fine)

50 ml hot water

10 g instant coffee granules

Caramel cream

50 g caster sugar (extra fine)

33 g whipping cream

$^1/_2$ Tbsp water

Filling

10 g unsalted butter

15 g honey

1 ripe medium banana, sliced

15 g raisins

1 tsp rum

1 Prepare joconde sponge. Preheat oven to 190°C. Prepare a 22 x 17-cm sheet of baking paper. Place on a baking tray.

2 Using an electric mixer with a whisk attachment, whisk egg white and caster sugar on high speed until stiff peaks form. Refrigerate until needed.

3 In another bowl, whisk egg, almond powder and icing sugar on high speed until batter reaches the ribbon stage. When you lift the whisk, the batter should fall slowly and form ribbons that hold their shape.

4 Fold $^1/_2$ of the meringue into the batter. Add flour and coffee granules, then mix well.

5 Add the remaining meringue and fold in using a spatula. Spread batter evenly on prepared baking paper. Bake for 7–8 minutes.

6 Transfer onto a wire rack and leave to cool. When joconde sponge is cooled, cut out two 10 x 15-cm rectangles. Set aside.

7 Prepare coffee essence. In a saucepan, melt sugar over medium heat until caramel in colour. While sugar is cooking, combine hot water and coffee granules. Remove syrup from heat and stir in coffee. Set aside.

8 Prepare caramel cream. In a saucepan, melt sugar over medium heat until caramel in colour. While sugar is cooking, combine whipping cream and water. Remove syrup from heat and stir in whipping cream mixture. Place in a baking pan filled with warm water.

9 Prepare chocolate pattern. Cover the back of a baking tray tightly with cling film. Melt 25 g chocolate in a heatproof bowl set over a pot of simmering water. Spread melted chocolate on prepared tray, using a comb to make a pattern. Place a 10 x 15-cm cake ring on top and refrigerate until needed.

10 Prepare filling. In a saucepan, combine butter and honey over medium heat. Add banana and raisins. Cook until banana slices are softened around the edges. Remove from heat, add rum and leave to cool.

4a

4b

5a

5b

6

Crème anglaise

8 g gelatine leaf

140 ml milk

1 egg yolk (20 g)

40 g caster sugar
(extra fine)

Mocha and caramel bavarois

200 g crème anglaise
(see above)

4 g instant coffee granules

40 g caramel cream
(see page 114)

160 g whipping cream

11 Prepare crème anglaise. Soak gelatine in a bowl of iced water for 20 minutes. Drain and squeeze to remove excess water. Set aside.

12 Heat milk in a saucepan over low heat. In a bowl, whisk egg yolk and sugar until pale. Remove warm milk and pour $\frac{1}{2}$ into egg yolk mixture. Whisk lightly to combine, then add egg yolk mixture to the remaining milk in the saucepan. Heat mixture, using a spatula to stir constantly until it thickens.

13 Remove from heat and add gelatine. Stir until gelatine is dissolved. Divide into two 100 g portions.

14 Prepare mocha and caramel bavarois. Add coffee granules to 1 portion of crème anglaise and mix well. Place in a baking pan filled with iced water to chill until slightly thickened.

15 In the meantime, whisk whipping cream on high speed until soft peaks form. Refrigerate until needed.

16 Add $\frac{1}{2}$ of whipping cream to chilled coffee mixture and mix well. Pour into rectangle cake ring and freeze for 5—10 minutes until the surface is firm.

17 Brush a joconde sponge layer with coffee essence. Place on top of mocha bavarois and brush with more coffee essence. Refrigerate while continuing to prepare caramel bavarois.

18 Add 40 g caramel cream to the other portion of crème anglaise. Gently fold in the remaining whipped cream, then pour $\frac{1}{2}$ of caramel bavarois into cake ring.

19 Add filling and spread evenly. Cover with the remaining caramel bavarois. Brush second joconde sponge layer with coffee essence, then place on top of caramel bavarois with the moistened side down.

20 Freeze for 4—5 hours until cake is set. To unmould, invert onto a tray and remove cake ring and cling film.

21 Brush top of cake with mirror gel, followed by coffee essence.

Printemps

Sakura Cake

All the flavours that represent spring in Japan inspired this cake.

Matcha biscuit

46 g cake flour

4 g matcha

2 egg yolks (40 g)

50 g caster sugar
(extra fine)

1$^1/_2$ egg whites (60 g)

Icing sugar for sprinkling

White bean mousse

4 g gelatine leaf

75 g whipping cream

75 ml milk

11 g caster sugar
(extra fine)

75 g white bean paste

Sakura mousse

3 g gelatine leaf

7 g salt pickled sakura
flowers, soaked in water
for 10 minutes

100 ml milk

33 g caster sugar
(extra fine)

Red food colouring, as
desired

2$^1/_2$ tsp water

1 egg white (30 g)

50 g whipping cream

1 tsp sakura liqueur

Sakura jelly

2 g gelatine leaf

3–4 salt pickled sakura
flowers, soaked in water
for 10 minutes

110 ml water

2 g caster sugar
(extra fine)

Red food colouring, as
desired

1 Tightly wrap the bottom of a 15-cm round cake ring with cling film. Prepare matcha biscuit. Preheat oven to 180°C. Line a 28-cm square baking tray. Sift cake flour and matcha together twice. Set aside.

2 In a bowl, beat egg yolks and 10 g caster sugar until pale. Using an electric mixer with a whisk attachment, whisk egg whites and the remaining caster sugar on high speed until stiff peaks form. Add egg yolk mixture to meringue and mix in gently.

3 Add flour mixture and fold in gently until just incorporated. Transfer to a piping bag fitted with a 12-mm round tip. Pipe batter diagonally on prepared baking tray. Sprinkle with icing sugar and leave to absorb into batter until no longer visible before sprinkling with icing sugar again. Bake for 10 minutes.

4 Remove onto a wire rack to cool. Cut a 13.5-cm circle, a 9-cm circle and 2 strips, each 3.5 x 20 cm, from cooled cookie sheet. Place the 13.5-cm circle inside the prepared cake ring and use the strips to line the sides.

5 Prepare white bean mousse. Soak gelatine in a bowl of iced water for 20 minutes. Drain and squeeze to remove excess water. Set aside.

6 Using an electric mixer with a whisk attachment, whisk whipping cream on high speed until soft peaks form. Refrigerate until needed.

7 In a saucepan, combine milk and sugar over medium heat until sugar is dissolved. Remove from heat, add white bean paste and mix well.

8 Microwave gelatine for 5–10 seconds. Add to milk mixture and mix well. Place in a baking pan filled with iced water to chill until slightly thickened.

9 Add whipping cream to chilled white bean mixture and fold in gently. Pour into cake ring and place the 9-cm biscuit circle on top. Refrigerate for 30–60 minutes until mousse is set.

10 Prepare sakura mousse. Soak gelatine in a bowl of iced water for 20 minutes. Drain and squeeze to remove excess water. Set aside.

11 Drain and squeeze sakura flowers to release excess water. Place in a blender and add milk, 10 g sugar and food colouring. Blend until combined, then transfer to a saucepan.

12 Heat over medium heat until just before mixture boils. Remove from heat, add gelatine and stir until gelatine is dissolved. Place in a baking pan filled with iced water to chill until slightly thickened.

13 Follow step 10 on page 81 to make Italian meringue with water, egg white and the remaining sugar. Leave to cool.

14 Using an electric mixer with a whisk attachment, whisk whipping cream on medium speed until soft peaks form. Add sakura liqueur and mix well. Add whipping cream to chilled sakura mixture.

15 Add $^1/_3$ of meringue to cream mixture and mix gently. Add this mixture to the remaining meringue, fold in gently and pour into cake ring. Refrigerate for 4–5 hours until mousse is set.

16 Prepare sakura jelly. Soak gelatine in a bowl of iced water for 20 minutes. Drain and squeeze to remove excess water. Set aside.

17 Drain sakura flowers and combine in a saucepan with water and sugar. Cook over medium heat until just before mixture boils. Remove from heat, then stir in gelatine and colouring. Place in a baking pan filled with iced water. Pour cooled jelly over mousse and refrigerate until jelly is set.

Ruby Lapis
Ruby Mousse Baumkuchen

This is an adaptation of a popular layer cake (*baumkuchen*) with a fluffy ruby chocolate topping.

120 g mirror gel

40 g raspberry purée,
at room temperature

Raspberry jelly

3 g gelatine leaf

90 g raspberry purée,
at room temperature

38 g caster sugar
(extra fine)

Baumkuchen

37 g cake flour

25 g cornstarch

1 g baking powder

10 g almond powder

5 g icing sugar

5 g egg white

56 g unsalted butter,
at room temperature

30 g maple syrup

A pinch of salt

1$^1/_2$ egg yolks (28 g),
at room temperature

2 tsp rum

Meringue

1 egg white (43 g)

29 g caster sugar
(extra fine)

Ruby chocolate mousse

2 g gelatine leaf

120 g whipping cream

85 g ruby chocolate

1 egg yolk (20 g)

35 g caster sugar
(extra fine)

8 tsp milk

1 tsp water

1 egg white (40 g)

1 Prepare raspberry jelly. Soak gelatine in a bowl of iced water for 20 minutes. Drain and squeeze to remove excess water. Microwave for 10 seconds. Add raspberry purée and sugar. Mix well and place bowl in a baking tray filled with iced water. Stir until mixture is thickened.

2 Line a 22 x 7-cm loaf tin with cling film. Transfer jelly mixture into loaf tin and freeze until jelly is set. Trim jelly into a 21 x 6-cm rectangle.

3 Prepare *baumkuchen*. Preheat oven to 230°C. Grease a 22 x 7-cm loaf tin and line the bottom with baking paper. Sift flour, cornstarch and baking powder together. Set aside.

4 Place almond powder and sugar in a bowl and mix using a spatula. Add egg white, stirring constantly until mixture clumps together. Add butter and mix until a paste forms.

5 Add maple syrup and salt, then whisk until fluffy. Gradually add egg yolks and mix well. Stir in rum and set aside.

6 Prepare meringue. Using an electric mixer with a whisk attachment, whisk egg whites on high speed. Gradually add sugar and whisk until stiff peaks form. Add $^1/_3$ of meringue into batter and mix well using a spatula. Fold in the remaining meringue. Gently fold flour mixture into batter.

7 Transfer to a piping bag. Pipe 35–40 g batter into prepared loaf tin, using a spatula to spread it evenly. Bake for 2–3 minutes, until surface is lightly browned. Remove from oven and place loaf tin on a wet tea towel to cool slightly. Repeat to pipe and cook more layers of cake until batter is used up. Bake the last layer for 4 minutes.

8 Remove onto a wire rack and leave cake to cool in loaf tin. Trim to fit a 24-cm yule log mould.

9 Prepare ruby chocolate mousse. Soak gelatine in a bowl of iced water for 20 minutes. Drain and squeeze to remove excess water.

10 Using an electric mixer with a whisk attachment, whisk whipping cream on high speed until soft peaks form. Refrigerate until needed.

11 Place ruby chocolate in a bowl. Using an electric mixer with a whisk attachment, whisk egg yolk and 25 g caster sugar on high speed until pale and thick. When you lift the whisk, the batter should fall slowly and form ribbons that hold their shape.

12 In a small saucepan, heat milk until just before it boils. Add milk to batter and mix. Return mixture to saucepan and heat until 83°C. Remove from heat, add gelatine and stir until gelatine is dissolved.

13 Strain mixture and add to ruby chocolate, whisking constantly to melt and incorporate chocolate. Leave to cool for a few minutes before folding in chilled whipping cream.

14 Follow step 10 on page 81 to make Italian meringue with water, egg white and the remaining sugar. Fold meringue into mousse.

15 To assemble, line a 24-cm yule log mould with cling film. Pour $^1/_2$ of mousse into mould. Top with raspberry jelly, followed by the remaining mousse and *baumkuchen*. Freeze until mousse is set.

16 To decorate, combine mirror gel and raspberry purée in a saucepan over low heat until 35°C. Unmould cake and pour glaze over mousse. Refrigerate until glaze is set.

Yoghurt Mousse Cake

The slight acidity of the yoghurt adds a refreshing tang to this mousse cake.

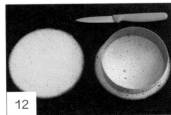

Makes one 15-cm round cake

2 slices 15-cm round genoise sponge, 1-cm thick (see page 19)

150 g whipping cream (optional)

12 g caster sugar (extra fine) (optional)

Blueberry jelly

2 g gelatine leaf

80 g blueberries

42 g caster sugar (extra fine)

1 Tbsp lemon juice

1 tsp water

Syrup

2 Tbsp water

10 g caster sugar (extra fine)

Yoghurt mousse

4 g gelatine leaf

145 g whipping cream

155 g Greek yoghurt

50 g caster sugar (extra fine)

1 Tbsp lemon juice

1 Tightly wrap a 12-cm round cake ring with cling film and place on a baking tray.

2 Prepare blueberry jelly. Soak gelatine in a bowl of iced water for 20 minutes. Drain and squeeze to remove excess water. Set aside.

3 Place blueberries, sugar, lemon juice and water in a blender. Blend until combined, then transfer to a saucepan. Heat over medium heat until mixture is 60°C.

4 Remove from heat, add gelatine and stir until gelatine is dissolved. Pour blueberry jelly mixture into prepared cake tin. Freeze for 2—3 hours until jelly is set.

5 Prepare syrup. Place water and sugar in a microwave-safe bowl and microwave in 10-second intervals until a syrup forms. Leave to cool.

6 Prepare yoghurt mousse. Soak gelatine in a bowl of iced water for 20 minutes. Drain and squeeze to remove excess water. Set aside.

7 Using an electric mixer with a whisk attachment, whisk whipping cream on high speed until soft peaks form. Refrigerate until needed.

8 Mix yoghurt, sugar and lemon juice in a bowl. Add 2 Tbsp yoghurt mixture to gelatine and microwave for 10—15 seconds until gelatine is dissolved.

9 Add gelatine mixture to the remaining yoghurt mixture. Place in a baking pan filled with iced water and stir constantly until mixture is slightly thickened.

10 Remove from baking pan, add whipping cream and fold in gently. Transfer yoghurt mousse to a piping bag.

11 Tightly wrap a 15-cm cake ring with cling film and place on a baking tray.

12 Use a 12-cm cake ring to cut a circle from each genoise sponge slice.

13 Place a genoise sponge circle into the prepared cake ring. Brush with syrup. Pipe a thin layer of yoghurt mousse into the ring and spread evenly. Place blueberry jelly on top of genoise sponge circle. Cover with another thin layer of yoghurt mousse. Top with second genoise sponge circle. Cover with the remaining mousse and spread evenly.

14 Refrigerate for 4—5 hours until mousse is set.

15 To unmould, wrap a warm towel around cake ring for a few seconds before lifting cake ring.

16 If desired, whisk whipping cream and sugar on high speed until firm peaks form. Pipe as desired to decorate cake.

13b

13c

13d

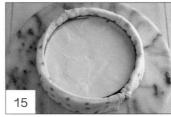
15

Coco Passion

Passion Fruit and Lemon Cheese Mousse Cake

This is such a fun cake to make because the combination of coconut and passion fruit makes me think of tropical island getaways.

4a

4b

4c

5

7

11a

11b

15

Biscuit sponge

45 g cake flour

25 g coconut milk
powder

2 egg whites (80 g)

50 g caster sugar
(extra fine)

2 egg yolks (35 g)

Icing sugar for sprinkling

Passion fruit mousse

4 g gelatine leaf

90 g whipping cream

90 g passion fruit purée,
at room temperature

13 g caster sugar

1 tsp orange liqueur

Coconut mousse

4 g gelatine leaf

125 g whipping cream

25 g caster sugar
(extra fine)

70 g cream cheese

30 g coconut purée

4 tsp lemon juice

Passion fruit jelly

30 g mirror gel

10 g passion fruit purée

1 Prepare biscuit sponge. Preheat oven to 190°C. On a large sheet of baking paper, draw a 15-cm circle, a 12-cm circle and a 6 x 30-cm rectangle, then line a baking tray with it.

2 Sift cake flour and coconut milk powder together twice. Set aside.

3 Using an electric mixer with a whisk attachment, whisk egg whites on high speed until voluminous. Add caster sugar in 2 equal portions, whisking well after each addition. Whisk until stiff peaks form.

4 Add egg yolks to meringue and whisk to incorporate. Gradually add flour mixture and fold in using a spatula until just incorporated. Transfer to a piping bag fitted with a 12-mm round tip. Pipe batter onto prepared baking tray according to the guides.

5 Sprinkle with icing sugar and leave to absorb into batter until no longer visible before sprinkling with icing sugar again. Bake for 9 minutes.

6 Remove from oven and leave to cool. Trim biscuit sponge pieces into a 14-cm circle, an 11-cm circle and two 2.5 x 26-cm rectangles.

7 Tightly wrap a 15-cm cake ring with cling film. Place 14-cm biscuit sponge circle into cake ring and line sides of ring with biscuit sponge rectangles. Set aside.

8 Prepare passion fruit mousse. Soak gelatine in a bowl of iced water for 20 minutes. Drain and squeeze to remove excess water.

9 Using an electric mixer with a whisk attachment, whisk whipping cream on high speed until soft peaks form. Refrigerate until needed.

10 In a saucepan, combine passion fruit purée and sugar over medium heat until 60°C. Remove from heat, add gelatine and stir until gelatine is dissolved. Add orange liqueur and mix well. Place in a baking pan filled with iced water until mixture thickens slightly.

11 Add whipping cream to chilled passion fruit mixture and mix to combine. Pour into prepared cake ring. Place 11-cm biscuit sponge circle on top. Refrigerate for 4–5 hours until mousse is set.

12 Prepare coconut cheese mousse. Soak gelatine in a bowl of iced water for 20 minutes. Drain and squeeze to remove excess water. Set aside.

13 Using an electric mixer with a whisk attachment, whisk whipping cream and sugar on high speed until soft peaks form. Refrigerate until needed.

14 Place cream cheese in a microwave-safe bowl and microwave for 30 seconds. In a saucepan, combine coconut purée and lemon juice over medium heat until mixture reaches 65°C. Remove from heat and gradually add to cream cheese, mixing to combine.

15 Microwave gelatine for 10–15 seconds until melted. Add to coconut cream cheese mixture and stir until gelatine is dissolved. Fold mixture into chilled whipping cream.

16 Pour into cake ring, ensuring that mousse fills the mould completely. Smooth over the surface, then refrigerate until mousse is set.

17 Prepare passion fruit jelly. Combine mirror gel and passion fruit purée in a bowl and mix well. Pour jelly on top of mousse and refrigerate to set. Unmould before serving.

Concorde

Cocoa Mousse Meringue Cake

This cake is my interpretation of a dessert originally
designed to celebrate the advent of supersonic travel.

20 g raspberry purée, at room temperature

6 g caster sugar

Cocoa powder for dusting

Chocolate meringue

4 egg whites (155 g)

195 g caster sugar (extra fine)

1/4 tsp lemon juice or vinegar

45 g cocoa powder

Chocolate mousse

3 g gelatine leaf

2 egg yolks (38 g)

5 tsp water

30 g caster sugar (extra fine)

120 g dark baking chocolate, melted

190 g whipping cream

1   Preheat oven to 120°C. On a large sheet of baking paper, draw three 14-cm circles, then line a baking tray with it. Line another baking tray.

2   Prepare chocolate meringue. Place egg whites and sugar in a heatproof bowl set over a pot of simmering water. Heat until mixture is 50°C, whisking constantly. Remove from heat and add lemon juice. Using an electric mixer with a whisk attachment, whisk on high speed until glossy stiff peaks form.

3   Sift cocoa powder into meringue and gently fold in using a spatula. Transfer to a piping bag fitted with a 10-mm round tip. Pipe three 14-cm meringue circles onto baking tray, using the guides and piping in spirals. Pipe the remaining meringue into long strips on the second baking tray.

4   Bake for 80 minutes. Leave in oven to cool completely.

5   Prepared chocolate mousse. Soak gelatine in a bowl of iced water for 20 minutes. Drain and squeeze to remove excess water. Set aside.

6   Combine egg yolks, water and sugar in a heatproof bowl set over a pot of boiling water. Heat until 83°C, remove from heat and add to chocolate. Mix lightly to combine.

7   Microwave gelatine for 5–10 seconds until melted. Add to mixture and stir until gelatine is dissolved. Leave to cool until room temperature.

8   Using an electric mixer with a whisk attachment, whisk whipping cream on high speed until soft peaks form. Add a few scoops of whipping cream to chocolate mixture and fold in gently. Add mixture to whipping cream and mix lightly to combine. Transfer to a piping bag. Set aside.

9   Combine raspberry purée with sugar and whisk well.

10 Tightly wrap a 15-cm cake ring with cling film. Place a meringue circle into the ring, ensuring that the flat side of the meringue is on the bottom. Brush with raspberry syrup. Pipe 1/3 of mousse into cake ring, covering the meringue completely. Repeat to layer meringue brushed with syrup and mousse twice, placing the last meringue with its flat side up. Smooth over final layer of mousse.

11 Refrigerate for 4–5 hours until mousse is set. To unmould, wrap a warm towel around cake ring for a few seconds before lifting cake ring.

12 Cut long meringue strips into 2- to 3-cm pieces. Press meringue pieces all over the sides and top of the cake, ensuring that the mousse surface is completely covered. Dust with cocoa powder before serving.

3a

3b

10a

10b

SOMETHING SPECIAL

Galette Des Rois Noir

Galette Des Rois Black Forest-style

My husband loves black forest cake, and this
interpretation of the traditional French pastry
cake never disappoints him.

7–10 stewed cherries or canned dark cherries, pitted and halved

Inverted puff pastry

200g unsalted butter, cut into cubes and chilled

30 g bread flour

50 g cake flour

Cocoa pastry

7 g salt

75 ml cold water

1 tsp white vinegar

60 g bread flour

115 g cake flour

6 g cocoa powder

50 g unsalted butter, melted

Chocolate almond cream

4 tsp water

10 g custard powder

50 g unsalted butter, at room temperature

50 g icing sugar

50 g almond powder (extra fine)

$^2/_3$ egg (40 g)

10 g kirschwasser (cherry liqueur)

50 g baking chocolate, finely chopped

1. Prepare inverted puff pastry. Place butter and both flours into a food processor bowl. Freeze for 30 minutes. Pulse chilled ingredients a few times until mixture is clumpy. Be careful not to over mix.

2. Transfer dough to a work surface covered with cling film and roll into a 20-cm square. Refrigerate for at least 2 hours.

3. Prepare cocoa pastry. Dissolve salt in cold water, then stir in vinegar.

4. In another bowl, combine flours, cocoa powder and butter. Use a spatula to stir until mixture resembles breadcrumbs. Gradually add salt water mixture, stirring constantly until combined.

5. Transfer pastry to a work surface covered with cling film and roll into a 15-cm square. Refrigerate for at least 2 hours.

6. On a work surface covered with cling film, roll inverted puff pastry evenly into a 30-cm square. Place cocoa pastry in the middle and wrap with puff pastry. Wrap in cling film and refrigerate for at least 3 hours, preferably overnight.

7. On a lightly floured surface, roll pastry to make a 20 x 40-cm sheet. Bring the short edges to meet in the middle, then fold pastry into half along the middle line, ensuring that the edges are aligned. Turn pastry 90° clockwise and repeat to roll out and fold pastry.

8. Repeat to turn and roll out pastry. Fold pastry into thirds. Wrap in cling film and refrigerate for at least 1 hour.

9. Prepare chocolate almond cream. Combine water and custard powder. Let sit for 5 minutes before mixing to form a smooth custard. Set aside.

10. In another bowl, beat butter on high speed until creamy. Add sugar and mix to combine.

11. Add almond powder and mix using a spatula. Gradually add egg, followed by kirschwasser, custard and baking chocolate, mixing well after each addition. Refrigerate for 1 hour before transferring to a piping bag.

12. Prepare egg wash. Place all ingredients for egg wash in a bowl and whisk well. Strain before setting aside.

6a

6b

7

8

13a

13b

Egg wash

$1/_3$ egg (20 g)

1 egg yolk (20 g)

A pinch of salt

A pinch of sugar

Syrup

50 ml water

65 g caster sugar
(extra fine)

13 On a work surface covered with cling film, cut chilled pastry into 2 portions, with 1 slightly larger portion. Refrigerate smaller portion and roll larger portion into a 21-cm square, about 5-mm thick. Drape pastry sheet over an 18-cm pie tin and gently press it in.

14 Pipe $2/_3$ of chocolate almond cream in a spiral to fill pie tin. Arrange cherry halves on top, then pipe remaining cream over. If making this for Epiphany, push the charm (*feve*) into the cream here. Refrigerate while preparing top pastry.

15 On a lightly floured surface, roll smaller portion of pastry into a 3-mm thick square that's slightly larger than the pie tin.

16 Remove pie tin from refrigerator and brush egg wash on pastry edges. Place second pastry sheet on top at a 45° angle to the first sheet. Gently push out any air between pastry sheets. Trim excess dough with a sharp knife. Refrigerate pie tin if pastry is soft.

17 Invert pie onto a sheet of baking paper. Crimp edges using the back of a knife, with about a thumb's width between each notch. Brush egg wash all over pastry, except the sides, and refrigerate for 30 minutes.

18 Brush pie with egg wash once more and refrigerate for another 30 minutes. Preheat oven to 200°C.

19 Line a baking tray with a silicone baking mat and transfer pie onto it. Score pie surface using the tip of a sharp knife. Use a skewer to punch small holes along the scoring. Adjust oven to 180°C and bake pie for 60 minutes.

20 Prepare sugar syrup. In a saucepan, combine sugar and water over medium heat until sugar is dissolved. When pie is done, remove from oven and brush immediately with syrup. Leave to cool.

> **TIP**
> An almond can be used as a substitute for the charm. Placing the top sheet of pastry at a 45°C angle helps the edges rise more evenly.

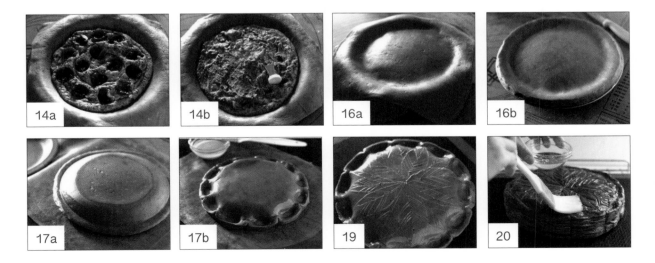

14a   14b   16a   16b

17a   17b   19   20

Mini Strawberry Paris-Brest

Not only do these smaller versions of a traditional Paris-Brest look cute, they are perfectly sized for an individual portion of dessert.

12 strawberries

Icing sugar for dusting

Choux pastry

8 tsp milk

60 ml water

40 g unsalted butter

A pinch of salt

40 g cake flour

20 g bread flour

2 eggs (100 g)

60–70 g sliced almonds

Custard cream

15 g cake flour

5 g cornstarch

40 g caster sugar
 (extra fine)

170 ml milk

2 egg yolks (40 g)

5-cm length vanilla bean

20 g unsalted butter, at
 room temperature, cut
 into small pieces

1 Prepare custard cream. Sift cake flour and cornstarch together. Add $^2/_3$ of sugar and mix evenly.

2 Add $^1/_4$ of milk to flour mixture and mix until flour is dissolved. Add egg yolks and whisk to incorporate. Set aside.

3 Split vanilla bean lengthwise. Using a paring knife, scrape seeds into a medium saucepan. Add the remaining milk and sugar, then bring to a boil.

4 Strain vanilla mixture and add to egg yolk mixture, whisking constantly to combine. Strain custard mixture into a clean saucepan. Bring to a boil over medium heat, whisking custard constantly as it thickens.

5 When a few bubbles break the surface, remove from heat and add butter pieces. Whisk until butter is incorporated. Transfer to a bowl placed in a baking pan filled with iced water. Stir constantly until custard cream is chilled, then cover with cling film and refrigerate until needed.

6 Prepare choux pastry. Preheat oven to 190ºC. Draw seven 7-cm circles to use as guides on a sheet of baking paper, then line a baking tray with it.

7 In a medium saucepan, combine milk, water, butter and salt over medium-high heat and heat until just before mixture boils. Remove from heat and add both flours. Using a wooden spoon, stir quickly to combine. Place over medium heat, stirring constantly until a film forms on the bottom of the saucepan.

8 Transfer milk mixture to a bowl. Add $^1/_2$ of eggs and stir vigorously to incorporate. To test if dough is done, scoop up $^1/_2$ of it using a spatula. The dough should fall back into the bowl within 3 seconds in a triangle shape. Gradually mix in the remaining eggs in portions until dough is the right consistency. You may not need to use all of the eggs. Reserve remaining egg to use as egg wash.

Strawberry cream

200 g whipping cream

16 g caster sugar
(extra fine)

30 g strawberry purée

9 While dough is warm, transfer to a piping bag fitted with a 10- or 12-mm round tip. Pipe a 7-cm ring on prepared baking tray, using a circle as a guide. Pipe a smaller ring inside the first ring, then pipe another ring on top. Repeat to make 6—7 circles.

10 Brush with egg wash and score lightly with flat tines of a wet fork. Sprinkle sliced almonds on top and spray circles with a little water. Bake for 10 minutes. Adjust oven to 170ºC and bake for 15 minutes.

11 Without opening oven door, leave baked choux pastries to sit in oven for 10 minutes, then remove onto a wire rack to cool completely.

12 Prepare strawberry cream. Using an electric mixer with a whisk attachment, whisk whipping cream and sugar on high speed until soft peaks form. Set 50 g aside for custard cream.

13 Add strawberry purée to the remaining whipping cream and whisk to mix. Transfer to a piping bag fitted with a star-shaped tip.

14 Lightly whisk chilled custard cream until smooth. Add reserved whipping cream and mix well before transferring to a piping bag.

15 To assemble, slice choux pastries horizontally about slightly less than $1/2$ from the top. Pipe custard cream on bottom halves. Pipe strawberry cream over custard cream, then arrange strawberries on top. Cover with pastry tops and dust with icing sugar.

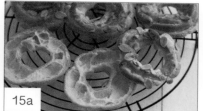

Cocoa Meringue Chantilly

This meringue dessert is so light that it is almost like eating a cloud.

30 g candied yuzu peels

Roasted almond slices for topping

Icing sugar for dusting

Salted caramel chantilly

230 g whipping cream

15 g glucose

40 g caster sugar (extra fine)

A pinch of salt

Cocoa meringue

10 g icing sugar

8 g cocoa powder

60 g caster sugar (extra fine)

4 tsp water

1 egg white (40 g)

1 Prepare salted caramel chantilly a day ahead. In a small saucepan, heat 70 g whipping cream until just before it boils. Meanwhile, combine glucose and 30 g sugar in a pot over medium heat. Heat until mixture caramelises. Remove from heat, add whipping cream and mix well. Stir in salt. Strain into a small bowl and leave to cool. Cover and refrigerate overnight.

2 Prepare cocoa meringue. Preheat oven to 110°C. Line a baking tray.

3 Sift icing sugar and cocoa powder together twice. Set aside.

4 Follow steps 1–4 to make Italian meringue (see page 21), using caster sugar, water and egg white. Continue whisking until meringue is slightly heavy and does not fall when its bowl is overturned.

5 Fold cocoa mixture into meringue before transferring to piping bag fitted with a 12-mm open star tip.

6 Pipe 4 small circles overlapping each other so that they form a wavy log. Repeat to make 12 logs. Bake for 120 minutes and leave in oven to cool completely.

7 Using an electric mixer with a whisk attachment, whisk the remaining whipping cream and sugar for salted caramel chantilly on high speed until soft peaks form. Using a spatula, fold in caramel mixture before transferring to a piping bag fitted with a 10-mm open star tip.

8 To assemble, pipe caramel chantilly onto a cocoa meringue and arrange a few candied yuzu peels on top. Cover with another meringue and turn meringue sandwich on its side. Pipe a layer of salted caramel chantilly on top, sprinkle with roasted almond slices and dust with icing sugar. Repeat to make 6 servings.

TIP

For the variation, substitute candied yuzu peel with candied orange peel or fresh raspberries.

Raspberry Guimauve Macaron

The raspberry flavour counters the sweetness of the meringue, making these macarons a popular treat. They are always the first to disappear from the dessert table.

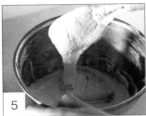

15 g raspberry jam

3 g cornstarch

3 g icing sugar

Macaron shells

100 g almond powder (extra fine)

100 g icing sugar

A few drops of food colouring

2 egg whites (74 g)

100 g caster sugar (extra fine)

2 Tbsp water

Raspberry guimauve

4 g gelatine leaf

30 g invert sugar

30 g raspberry purée

42 g caster sugar

1 Preheat oven to 180°C. Draw 60 circles, each about 3–3.5 cm, to use as guides on a sheet of baking paper. Line a baking tray with it. Fit a piping bag with a 10-mm round tip.

2 Prepare macaron shells. Sift almond powder and icing sugar together 3 times.

3 In another bowl, combine food colouring and ½ of egg whites. Mix well before adding almond powder mixture. Set aside.

4 Follow steps 1–4 to make Italian meringue (see page 21) using sugar, water and the remaining egg white. Whisk meringue until 50°C.

5 Add meringue to almond mixture and fold in using a spatula. While folding almond mixture in, push batter against the sides of the bowl before scooping it up from the bottom. Mix until batter is evenly mixed and falls back into the bowl in thick ribbons.

6 Transfer to prepared piping bag and pipe on prepared baking tray, using circles as guides. Tap baking tray lightly against a hard surface to release any bubbles. Leave piped batter to sit until the tops are dry to the touch.

7 Bake for 3 minutes until feet (*epi*) develop. Adjust oven to 130°C and place an empty baking sheet on the middle oven rack to help prevent macaron shells from browning. Bake for 10–12 minutes.

8 Remove from oven and transfer macarons with baking paper onto a wire rack. Leave to cool completely before lifting macarons off baking paper.

9 Prepare raspberry *guimauve*. Soak gelatine in a bowl of iced water for 20 minutes. Drain and squeeze to remove excess water. Place gelatine in a mixing bowl with 15 g invert sugar.

10 In a saucepan, combine raspberry purée, caster sugar and the remaining invert sugar, then heat until 110°C. Add to gelatine mixture.

11 Using an electric mixer with a whisk attachment, whisk mixture on low speed to combine. Adjust speed to high and whisk until stiff peaks form and mixture does not fall when its bowl is overturned. Transfer to a piping bag fitted with a 7- to 10-mm round tip.

12 While raspberry *guimauve* is warm, pipe onto a macaron shell in a ring and fill its centre with raspberry jam. Sandwich with another macaron shell. Repeat to make 30 macarons.

13 Mix cornstarch and icing sugar together, then brush on sides of macarons. Refrigerate for 24 hours before serving.

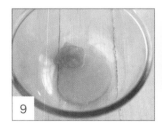

Triple Green

Those who love all things green tea will enjoy these cakes.

Matcha genoise sponge

75 g cake flour

7 g matcha

15 g unsalted butter

4$\frac{1}{2}$ tsp milk

4 eggs (155 g)

80 g caster sugar
   (extra fine)

20 g glucose

**Baked matcha
cheesecake**

20 g white baking
   chocolate

210 g cream cheese

80 g caster sugar

160 g plain unsweetened
   yoghurt

1 egg (50 g)

16 g cornstarch, sifted

8 g matcha, sifted

160 g whipping cream

1 Prepare matcha genoise sponge. Sift cake flour and matcha together twice. Follow steps 1—8 to make genoise sponge (see page 19). Slice cake horizontally to get 2 round sponge slices, each 1- to 1.5-cm thick.

2 Prepare baked matcha cheesecake. Preheat oven to 190°C. Wrap the base of two 15-cm round cake tins with foil and place a sponge slice in each tin.

3 Melt chocolate in a heatproof bowl set over a pot of simmering water. Set aside.

4 Place cream cheese in a microwave-safe bowl and microwave until softened. Add to a blender with sugar and yoghurt, then pulse to mix. Add egg, cornstarch, matcha and whipping cream, blending well after each addition.

5 Strain batter and pour equally into prepared tins. Bake for 10 minutes before adjusting oven to 160°C and baking for 20 minutes. Leave to cool completely in cake tin.

6 Prepare no-bake matcha cheesecake. Soak gelatine in a bowl of iced water for 20 minutes. Drain and squeeze to remove excess water.

7 In a small bowl, place matcha and add hot water. Whisk well to make a paste.

8 Place cream cheese in a heatproof bowl set over a pot of simmering water until softened. Remove from heat, add yoghurt, whipping cream, sugar and lemon juice, mixing well after each addition. Place in a baking pan filled with warm water.

9 Microwave gelatine for 5—10 seconds until melted. Add to cream cheese batter and mix well. Strain batter twice.

No-bake matcha cheesecake

12 g gelatine leaf

15 g matcha, sifted

60 ml hot water

250 g cream cheese

140 g plain unsweetened yoghurt

210 g whipping cream

60 g caster sugar

1 Tbsp lemon juice

10 Divide batter into 2 equal portions.

11 For 1 portion, set aside 50 g and two portions of 90 g. Add a little matcha paste to a 90 g portion, increasing the amount added to the other 90 g portion, followed by the 50 g portion. Reserve some matcha paste for the second cake.

12 Run a knife between the edge of the baked cheesecake and its cake tin to loosen it slightly. Pour plain cream cheese batter into cake tin. Pouring from the centre, add matcha batter from lightest to darkest to create an ombre effect. Refrigerate until cake is set.

13 Divide second portion of cream cheese batter into 2, using a ratio of 1:4. Mix the remaining matcha paste into the smaller portion.

14 Run a knife between the edge of the second baked cheesecake and its cake tin to loosen it slightly. Pour plain cream cheese batter into cake tin. To create a marble effect, drop matcha batter in teaspoonfuls on top and drag a skewer through to make a swirl pattern. Refrigerate until cake is set.

12a

12b

14a

14b

14c

Striped Coffee Jelly

This is a delicious treat for coffee lovers. Who doesn't love jello?

Makes 3 servings

Milk jelly

24 g caster sugar
(extra fine)

5 g agar powder

140 ml milk

140 g whipping cream

Coffee milk jelly

24g caster sugar
(extra fine)

5 g agar powder

280 ml milk

5 g instant coffee
granules

Coffee jelly

12 g caster sugar
(extra fine)

5 g agar powder

280 ml water

8 g instant coffee
granules

1 Prepare 3 glass pudding jars.

2 Prepare milk jelly. Place sugar and agar powder in a bowl and mix well.

3 In a saucepan, combine agar mixture, milk and whipping cream over medium heat. Bring to a gentle boil, then lower heat to let mixture simmer for about 1 minute, stirring constantly until agar is dissolved.

4 Slowly pour 25 g of milk jelly mixture into each pudding jar. Use a toothpick to pop any bubbles, then refrigerate until jelly is set. Place the remaining milk jelly mixture in a baking pan filled with warm water.

5 Prepare coffee milk jelly. Place sugar and agar powder in a bowl and mix well.

6 In a saucepan, combine agar mixture, milk and instant coffee granules over medium heat. Bring to a gentle boil, then lower heat to let mixture simmer for about 1 minute, stirring constantly until agar is dissolved.

7 Slowly pour 25 g of coffee milk jelly mixture into each pudding jar, covering milk jelly layer. Use a toothpick to pop any bubbles, then refrigerate until jelly is set. Place the remaining coffee milk jelly mixture in a baking pan filled with warm water.

8 Prepare coffee jelly. Place sugar and agar powder in a bowl and mix well.

9 In a saucepan, combine agar mixture and water over medium heat. Bring to a gentle boil and add instant coffee granules. Mix well, then lower heat to let mixture simmer for about 1 minute, stirring constantly until agar is dissolved.

10 Slowly pour 25 g of coffee jelly mixture into each pudding jar, covering coffee milk jelly layer. Use a toothpick to pop any bubbles, then refrigerate until jelly is set. Place the remaining coffee jelly mixture in a baking pan filled with warm water.

11 Repeat to layer milk jelly, coffee milk jelly and coffee jelly until pudding jars are filled. Pour each new layer along the wall of each pudding jar to prevent mixing with the lower layers. Refrigerate for 5 minutes after adding each new layer to let it set.

> **TIP**
> To avoid agar powder lumps in the jelly mixtures, mix agar powder with sugar immediately after measuring it out. Whisk the jelly mixture well before adding a new layer to the jars.

Wreath Tart

Wreaths are often used for decoration during the festive season, so this tart is the perfect edible table decoration.

100 g whipping cream

8 g caster sugar
(extra fine)

15 g mascarpone
cheese

Icing sugar for dusting

Fresh fruits for
decorating

Fresh mint for garnishing

Tart shell

60 g unsalted butter, cut
into cubes and chilled

37 g icing sugar

15 g almond powder
(extra fine)

$^1/_3$ egg (20 g)

110 g cake flour

Almond cream

35 g unsalted butter, at
room temperature

35g caster sugar
(extra fine)

$^1/_2$ egg (35 g)

35 g almond powder
(extra fine)

6 g cornstarch

5 g custard powder

1. Prepare almond cream. Follow steps 1–3 to make almond cream (see page 21).

2. Prepare tart shell. Follow steps 1–5 to make basic tart shell (see page 20).

3. Drape dough over an 18-cm tart tin and gently press it in. Trim the edges.

4. Combine dough trimmings and roll into a 24 x 2-cm rectangle. Wrap dough around the outside of a 7-cm round mousse ring, ensuring that dough is about 3 mm from the ring's edge. Place mousse ring firmly in the centre of tart tin, then remove dough inside of the ring.

5. Poke holes in tart shell using a fork before piping almond cream into tart. Refrigerate while preheating oven.

6. Preheat oven to 170°C.

7. Bake for 30 minutes. Unmould and leave to cool completely on a wire rack.

8. Using an electric mixer with a whisk attachment, whisk whipping cream and 4 g caster sugar on high speed until firm peaks form.

9. In a separate bowl, whisk mascarpone cheese and the remaining caster sugar until sugar is incorporated. Add to whipping cream and mix to combine. Transfer to a piping bag.

10. Pipe cream onto tart as desired to decorate, then lightly dust icing sugar on edge of tart. Decorate with fruits and mint leaves as desired.

7

10a

10b

Engadiner

Swiss Nut Tart

The dried pineapple gives a lovely tropical twist to this traditional tart filled with nuts and caramel.

Tart shell

100 g unsalted butter, cut into cubes and chilled

60 g icing sugar

25 g almond powder (extra fine)

1/2 egg (30 g)

185 g cake flour

Zest of 1/2 organic lemon

A pinch of salt

Nut filling

80 g caster sugar (extra fine)

96 g whipping cream

15 g unsalted butter

25 g honey

110 g roasted walnuts, chopped

45 g dried pineapple chunks, rinsed, dried and chopped into chunks

2 tsp brandy

Egg wash

1/2 egg yolk

1/8 tsp milk

1/8 tsp coffee

1. Prepare tart shell. Follow steps 1–3 to make basic tart shell (see page 21). Add lemon zest and salt to flour before combining with butter mixture.

2. Transfer dough to a work surface covered with cling film. Divide dough into 2 portions, using a ratio of 2:3.

3. Roll larger portion into a 25-cm circle. Drape over an 18-cm tart tin and gently press it in. Roll smaller portion into a 22-cm circle and place on a baking sheet. Refrigerate tart shell and dough circle until needed.

4. Prepare nut filling. Line a baking tray. In a medium saucepan, combine sugar, whipping cream, butter and honey over medium heat until mixture is 118°C. Add walnuts, dried pineapple and brandy. Stir to combine, then remove from heat.

5. Pour nut filling onto prepared tray and spread into a 16-cm circle. Leave to cool, then refrigerate for 5 minutes before using.

6. Preheat oven to 180°C.

7. Prepare egg wash. In a small bowl, combine egg yolk, milk and coffee.

8. To assemble, place nut filling in tart shell and cover with dough circle. Seal tart and trim the edges before brushing with egg wash. Score tart surface using the tip of a sharp knife, making sure not to cut through tart dough. Use a skewer to punch small holes along the scoring.

9. Bake for 35 minutes. Remove from oven, cover tart with foil and bake for another 10 minutes. Transfer onto a wire rack to cool completely in tart tin.

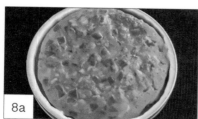

Flower Sugar Cubes

This adds a nice touch to the sugar you take with your post-meal coffee or tea.

Makes 15 cubes

2 g dried egg white powder

2½ tsp water

80 g icing sugar

A few drops of red and green food colouring

15 sugar cubes

1 In a bowl, combine egg white powder and water. Leave to sit for 5 minutes until egg white powder is dissolved.

2 Combine egg white mixture with icing sugar, then mix until icing is stiff and can hold its shape when lifted with a spatula.

3 Divide icing into 2 portions, using the ratio 1:3. Cover the smaller portion with cling film.

4 Add red food colouring to the larger portion of icing and mix to incorporate evenly. Transfer to a piping bag fitted with a small petal tip. I use a Wilton #101 tip.

5 Moving the tip in a small circle, pipe a small mound on a sugar cube to form the bud. Hold the fatter end of the piping tip closer to the bud, then pipe a petal on one side of the bud by moving the tip in a small arc. Pipe 2 more petals to cover the bud. Add more petals as desired to form a rose. Repeat to pipe on all 10 sugar cubes.

6 Add green food colouring to the smaller portion of icing and mix to incorporate evenly. Transfer to a piping bag without a piping tip, then cut the tip of the piping bag at a right angle.

7 Hold the tip so that the notch opens out onto the sides. Position the tip close to the base of a rose, then pipe a leaf by wiggling the tip back and forth to form a ridged triangle. Add more leaves as desired. Repeat to pipe on all 10 sugar cubes.

Weights and Measures

Quantities for this book are given in Metric and American (spoon and cup) measures. Standard spoon and cup measurements used are: 1 teaspoon = 5 ml, 1 tablespoon = 15 ml, 1 cup = 250 ml. All measures are level unless otherwise stated.

LIQUID AND VOLUME MEASURES

Metric	Imperial	American
5 ml	$1/6$ fl oz	1 teaspoon
10 ml	$1/3$ fl oz	1 dessertspoon
15 ml	$1/2$ fl oz	1 tablespoon
60 ml	2 fl oz	$1/4$ cup (4 tablespoons)
85 ml	$2^{1}/_{2}$ fl oz	$1/3$ cup
90 ml	3 fl oz	$3/8$ cup (6 tablespoons)
125 ml	4 fl oz	$1/2$ cup
180 ml	6 fl oz	$3/4$ cup
250 ml	8 fl oz	1 cup
300 ml	10 fl oz ($1/2$ pint)	$1^{1}/_{4}$ cups
375 ml	12 fl oz	$1^{1}/_{2}$ cups
435 ml	14 fl oz	$1^{3}/_{4}$ cups
500 ml	16 fl oz	2 cups
625 ml	20 fl oz (1 pint)	$2^{1}/_{2}$ cups
750 ml	24 fl oz ($1^{1}/_{5}$ pints)	3 cups
1 litre	32 fl oz ($1^{3}/_{5}$ pints)	4 cups
1.25 litres	40 fl oz (2 pints)	5 cups
1.5 litres	48 fl oz ($2^{2}/_{5}$ pints)	6 cups
2.5 litres	80 fl oz (4 pints)	10 cups

DRY MEASURES

Metric	Imperial
30 grams	1 ounce
45 grams	$1^{1}/_{2}$ ounces
55 grams	2 ounces
70 grams	$2^{1}/_{2}$ ounces
85 grams	3 ounces
100 grams	$3^{1}/_{2}$ ounces
110 grams	4 ounces
125 grams	$4^{1}/_{2}$ ounces
140 grams	5 ounces
280 grams	10 ounces
450 grams	16 ounces (1 pound)
500 grams	1 pound, $1^{1}/_{2}$ ounces
700 grams	$1^{1}/_{2}$ pounds
800 grams	$1^{3}/_{4}$ pounds
1 kilogram	2 pounds, 3 ounces
1.5 kilograms	3 pounds, $4^{1}/_{2}$ ounces
2 kilograms	4 pounds, 6 ounces

OVEN TEMPERATURE

	°C	°F	Gas Regulo
Very slow	120	250	1
Slow	150	300	2
Moderately slow	160	325	3
Moderate	180	350	4
Moderately hot	190/200	370/400	5/6
Hot	210/220	410/440	6/7
Very hot	230	450	8
Super hot	250/290	475/550	9/10

LENGTH

Metric	Imperial
0.5 cm	$1/4$ inch
1 cm	$1/2$ inch
1.5 cm	$3/4$ inch
2.5 cm	1 inch